D0846392

What People Are Saying about *Threshold Bible Study*

"This fine series will deepen your understanding of Scripture, but most importantly it can deepen your faith. In the classical tradition of *lectio divina*, this series also offers a very practical way to equip people for the New Evangelization."

ARCHBISHOP CHARLES J. CHAPUT, OFM CAP, *Archbishop of Philadelphia*

"With lucidity and creativity, Stephen Binz offers today's believing communities a rich and accessible treasury of biblical scholarship. The series' brilliance lies in its simplicity of presentation complemented by critical depth of thought and reflective insight."

CAROL J. DEMPSEY, OP, *Associate Professor of Theology, University of Portland, OR*

"I am grateful for this new series introducing our Catholic people to the riches of Sacred Scripture. May these guides to understanding the great truths of our Redemption bring us all closer to the Lord of our salvation."

CARDINAL TIMOTHY DOLAN, *Archbishop of New York*

"The Church has called Scripture a 'font' and 'wellspring' for the spiritual life. *Threshold Bible Study* is one of the best sources for tapping into the biblical font. *Threshold Bible Study* offers you an encounter with the word that will make your heart come alive."

TIM GRAY, *President of the Augustine Institute, Denver*

"*Threshold Bible Study* offers solid scholarship and spiritual depth. It can be counted on for lively individual study and prayer, even while it offers spiritual riches to deepen communal conversation and reflection among the people of God."

SCOTT HAHN, *Founder and President of the St. Paul Center for Biblical Theology*

"*Threshold Bible Study* offers those who want to begin faith-filled and prayerful study of the Bible with a user-friendly tool. These books will open readers to a new and stimulating way to encounter the word of God."

LESLIE J. HOPPE, OFM, *Professor, Catholic Theological Union, Chicago*

"Stephen Binz has an amazing gift for making the meaning of the biblical text come alive! With a strong background in Bible study, he knows how to provide the roadmap any group can use to explore Scripture. I'd like to see this in the hands of every adult Catholic in the church today." ▦ **BILL HUEBSCH**, *author and theologian*

"Though the distance many feel between the word of God and their everyday lives can be overwhelming, it need not be so. *Threshold Bible Study* is a fine blend of the best of biblical scholarship and a realistic sensitivity to the spiritual journey of the believing Christian. I recommend it highly."
▦ **FRANCIS J. MOLONEY, SDB**, *Professor, Catholic University of Australia*

"*Threshold Bible Study* is appropriately named, for its commentary and study questions bring people to the threshold of the text and invite them in. The questions guide but do not dominate. Stephen Binz's work stands in the tradition of the biblical renewal movement and brings it back to life."
▦ **KATHLEEN M. O'CONNOR**, *Professor Emerita, Columbia Theological Seminary*

"I most strongly recommend this series, exceptional for its scholarly solidity, pastoral practicality, and clarity of presentation. The church owes Binz a great debt of gratitude for his generous and competent labor in the service of the word of God."
▦ **PETER C. PHAN**, *Professor of Catholic Social Thought, Georgetown University*

"*Threshold Bible Study* is an enriching and enlightening approach to understanding the rich faith which the Scriptures hold for us today. All the elements work together to offer the reader a wonderful insight into how the sacred texts of our faith can touch our lives in a profound and practical way today. I heartily recommend this series both to individuals and to Bible study groups."
▦ **ABBOT GREGORY J. POLAN, OSB**,
Conception Abbey, Abbot Primate of the Benedictine Order

"Stephen Binz has put together a great aid for Catholics hungering for Scripture study and application in their daily lives. *Threshold Bible Study* promises to help meet that need."
▦ **JOHN MICHAEL TALBOT**, *Catholic Christian Recording Artist, Little Portion Hermitage*

"*Threshold Bible Study* is that rare kind of program that will help one cross an elusive threshold—using the Bible effectively for prayer and spiritual enrichment. This user-friendly program will enhance any personal or group Bible study. Guaranteed to make your love of Scripture grow!"
▦ **RONALD D. WITHERUP, SS**, *Superior General of the Sulpicians, Paris*

MISSIONARY DISCIPLESHIP

THRESHOLD
BIBLE STUDY

MISSIONARY
DISCIPLESHIP

Stephen J. Binz

**TWENTY-THIRD
PUBLICATIONS**
twentythirdpublications.com

TWENTY-THIRD PUBLICATIONS
A division of Bayard
One Montauk Avenue, Suite 200
New London, CT 06320
(860) 437-3012 or (800) 321-0411
www.twentythirdpublications.com

Copyright ©2017 Stephen J. Binz. All rights reserved. No part of this publication may be reproduced in any manner without prior written permission of the publisher. Write to the Permissions Editor.

The Scripture passages contained herein are from the *New Revised Standard Version Bible*, Catholic edition. Copyright ©1989, by the Division of Christian Education of the National Council of the Churches of Christ in the U.S.A. All rights reserved.

ISBN: 978-1-62785-313-2
Library of Congress Control Number: 2017942546
Printed in the U.S.A.

Contents

LESSONS 13–18

LESSONS 19–24

LESSONS 25–30

How to Use
Threshold Bible Study

Each book in the *Threshold Bible Study* series is designed to lead you through a new doorway of biblical awareness, to accompany you across a unique threshold of understanding. The characters, places, and images that you encounter in each of these topical studies will help you explore fresh dimensions of your faith and discover richer insights for your spiritual life.

Threshold Bible Study covers biblical themes in depth in a short amount of time. Unlike more traditional Bible studies that treat a biblical book or series of books, *Threshold Bible Study* aims to address specific topics within the entire Bible. The goal is not for you to comprehend everything about each passage, but rather for you to understand what a variety of passages from different books of the Bible reveals about the topic of each study.

Threshold Bible Study offers you an opportunity to explore the entire Bible from the viewpoint of a variety of different themes. The commentary that follows each biblical passage launches your reflection about that passage and helps you begin to see its significance within the context of your contemporary experience. The questions following the commentary challenge you to understand the passage more fully and apply it to your own life. The prayer starter helps conclude your study by integrating learning into your relationship with God.

These studies are designed for maximum flexibility. Each study is presented in a workbook format, with sections for reading, reflecting, writing, discussing, and praying. Space for writing after each question is ideal for personal study and allows group members to prepare in advance for their discussion. The thirty lessons in each topic may be used by an individual over the period of a month, or by a group for six sessions, with lessons to be studied each week before the next group meeting. These studies are ideal for Bible study groups, small Christian communities, adult faith formation, student groups, Sunday school, neighborhood groups, and family reading, as well as for individual learning.

The method of *Threshold Bible Study* is rooted in the classical tradition of *lectio divina*, an ancient yet contemporary means for reading the Scriptures reflectively and prayerfully. Reading and interpreting the text (*lectio*) is followed by reflective meditation on its message (*meditatio*). This reading and reflecting flows into prayer from the heart (*oratio* and *contemplatio*).

This ancient method assures us that Bible study is a matter of both the mind and the heart. It is not just an intellectual exercise to learn more and be able to discuss the Bible with others. It is, more importantly, a transforming experience. Reflecting on God's word, guided by the Holy Spirit, illumines the mind with wisdom and stirs the heart with zeal.

Following the personal Bible study, *Threshold Bible Study* offers a method for extending *lectio divina* into a weekly conversation with a small group. This communal experience will allow participants to enhance their appreciation of the message and build up a spiritual community (*collatio*). The end result will be to increase not only individual faith but also faithful witness in the context of daily life (*operatio*).

Through the spiritual disciplines of Scripture reading, study, reflection, conversation, and prayer, you will experience God's grace more abundantly as your life is rooted more deeply in Christ. The risen Jesus said: "Listen! I am standing at the door, knocking; if you hear my voice and open the door, I will come in to you and eat with you, and you with me" (Rev 3:20). Listen to the Word of God, open the door, and cross the threshold to an unimaginable dwelling with God!

SUGGESTIONS FOR INDIVIDUAL STUDY

- Make your Bible reading a time of prayer. Ask for God's guidance as you read the Scriptures.

- Try to study daily, or as often as possible according to the circumstances of your life.

- Read the Bible passage carefully, trying to understand both its meaning and its personal application as you read. Some persons find it helpful to read the passage aloud.

- Read the passage in another Bible translation. Each version adds to your understanding of the original text.

- Allow the commentary to help you comprehend and apply the scriptural text. The commentary is only a beginning, not the last word, on the meaning of the passage.

- After reflecting on each question, write out your responses. The very act of writing will help you clarify your thoughts, bring new insights, and amplify your understanding.

- As you reflect on your answers, think about how you can live God's word in the context of your daily life.

- Conclude each daily lesson by reading the prayer and continuing with your own prayer from the heart.

- Make sure your reflections and prayers are matters of both the mind and the heart. A true encounter with God's word is always a transforming experience.

- Choose a word or a phrase from the lesson to carry with you throughout the day as a reminder of your encounter with God's life-changing word.

- Share your learning experience with at least one other person whom you trust for additional insights and affirmation. The ideal way to share learning is in a small group that meets regularly.

SUGGESTIONS FOR GROUP STUDY

- Meet regularly; weekly is ideal. Try to be on time and make attendance a high priority for the sake of the group. The average group meets for about an hour.

- Open each session with a prepared prayer, a song, or a reflection. Find some appropriate way to bring the group from the workaday world into a sacred time of graced sharing.

- If you have not been together before, name tags are very helpful as a group begins to become acquainted with the other group members.

- Spend the first session getting acquainted with one another, reading the Introduction aloud, and discussing the questions that follow.

- Appoint a group facilitator to provide guidance to the discussion. The role of facilitator may rotate among members each week. The facilitator simply keeps the discussion on track; each person shares responsibility for the group. There is no need for the facilitator to be a trained teacher.

- Try to study the six lessons on your own during the week. When you have done your own reflection and written your own answers, you will be better prepared to discuss the six scriptural lessons with the group. If you have not had an opportunity to study the passages during the week, meet with the group anyway to share support and insights.

- Participate in the discussion as much as you are able, offering your thoughts, insights, feelings, and decisions. You learn by sharing with others the fruits of your study.

- Be careful not to dominate the discussion. It is important that everyone in the group be offered an equal opportunity to share the results of their work. Try to link what you say to the comments of others so that the group remains on the topic.

- When discussing your own personal thoughts or feelings, use "I" language. Be as personal and honest as appropriate and be very cautious about giving advice to others.

- Listen attentively to the other members of the group so as to learn from their insights. The words of the Bible affect each person in a different way, so a group provides a wealth of understanding for each member.

- Don't fear silence. Silence in a group is as important as silence in personal study. It allows individuals time to listen to the voice of God's Spirit and the opportunity to form their thoughts before they speak.

- Solicit several responses for each question. The thoughts of different people will build on the answers of others and will lead to deeper insights for all.

- Don't fear controversy. Differences of opinions are a sign of a healthy and honest group. If you cannot resolve an issue, continue on, agreeing to disagree. There is probably some truth in each viewpoint.

- Discuss the questions that seem most important for the group. There is no need to cover all the questions in the group session.

- Realize that some questions about the Bible cannot be resolved, even by experts. Don't get stuck on some issue for which there are no clear answers.

- Whatever is said in the group is said in confidence and should be regarded as such.

- Pray as a group in whatever way feels comfortable. Pray for the members of your group throughout the week.

Schedule for Group Study

SESSION 1: INTRODUCTION   DATE: _____

SESSION 2: LESSONS 1–6   DATE: _____

SESSION 3: LESSONS 7–12   DATE: _____

SESSION 4: LESSONS 13–18   DATE: _____

SESSION 5: LESSONS 19–24   DATE: _____

SESSION 6: LESSONS 25–30   DATE: _____

Always be ready to make your defense to anyone who demands from you an accounting for the hope that is in you; yet do it with gentleness and reverence. 1 PET 3:15–16

Missionary Discipleship

The mission of the church is to make known the person and message of Jesus Christ. As disciples of the Lord, all of us have been invited to play an active part in this mission. By word and witness, we are called to contribute to spreading the gospel, the good news of Jesus, to the world. If we are to be true to our identity as disciples, then we must be evangelizers, witnesses of the gospel to others.

There is an intimate connection between the word of God and the call to missionary discipleship. As we learn to listen to Scripture, we learn how to witness to the word of God. The more we receive that divine word into our hearts, the more our lives will reflect that word to the world. Discipleship is a call to go inward, to experience an ever-deepening encounter with Jesus Christ, and a call to go outward, to witness the good news to others.

The church is missionary by its very nature. Carrying on the mission of Jesus to the world, the church bears witness to the kingdom of God. Like Jesus, his community of disciples is called to continually make all things new, embodying the presence of Jesus through his Spirit in the world. A church that always looks inwardly, to its own internal issues and struggles, is a church that has forsaken its missionary vocation. A renewed and vibrant church must be outward-looking, evangelizing with zeal, living the gospel with joy and hope for the sake of the world.

In our day, the Holy Spirit through the church is calling followers of Jesus Christ to be soaked in the word of God so that we can be heralds of the gospel to the world. The more we become biblical disciples, the more we will become missionary disciples. Our vocation to evangelize cannot be delegated to others. Through baptism we become bearers of Christ, and in the Eucharist we become the body of Christ, so we witness him wherever we go.

The gospel offers us a whole new way of seeing the world, a fuller vision of our own lives and the lives of one another. While we can never impose the good news of God's love in Jesus Christ, we are called to bring it to others and let them know the beauty of life in Christ. We must resist the tendency to treat our convictions as a private matter. Our faith is not a costume that we put on for particular occasions. Only when faith permeates every aspect of our lives can we truly open the hearts of others to the transforming power of the gospel.

Reflection and discussion

- What are the implications of being a missionary disciple of Jesus Christ?

- Why does an inwardly focused church fail to fulfill its calling?

Obstacles to Hearing and Witnessing God's Word Today

The task of missionary discipleship is particularly difficult today because of the obstructions presented by our cultural setting. Although the message of the gospel remains the same—"Jesus Christ is the same yesterday and today and forever" (Heb 13:8)—the challenges of evangelization differ in every age. Here are a few of the obstacles to God's word being implanted in the minds and hearts of individuals and society today.

The first is secularism: living as if there were no God or any need for God. This secularism fosters a mentality in which God is simply left out of human consciousness and culture. Today we have crossed from a neutrality toward religion to hostility toward religion and denial of the transcendent truths upon which traditional society has been based. Divinely revealed truth is something that believers today are encouraged to experience within their own private lives but to leave out of the public domain. Anything that is above or beyond the present, practical world is not a matter for consideration in public life. Ultimate human purpose and destiny are beyond the purview of the secular culture. This increasing secularization has resulted in a declining capacity for people to listen and understand the words of the gospel as a true and life-giving message.

A second obstacle to missionary discipleship is rationalism, which holds that human reason is the sole arbiter and the final test of all truth. Of course, Christian theology has always defended the importance of reason, in alliance with faith, in seeking truth. But human reason, divorced from faith, cannot know the highest forms of truth, which are knowable only through divine revelation. The supernatural gift of faith permits us to experience God in ways that reason alone cannot.

A third obstruction to hearing and witnessing God's word is relativism, which holds that there is no absolute truth or value. All ideas have only relative, subjective value according to personal differences in perception and judgment. In today's culture, the truths of faith tend to be viewed as merely personal opinions. But Christian faith rests in the certainty of God's revealing word. It is a faith that does not follow the waves of trends and the latest novelties. It gives us the knowledge to judge truth from deceit. We cannot truly hear God's word unless we trust that it expresses divine truth, and we cannot witness to God's word unless we know that it is not subject to changeable opinion and personal whim.

A fourth obstacle today is individualism. Human life no longer has a purpose that is commonly agreed upon or a conception of the good toward which human life ought to aim. So individuals are free to choose their own personal values and live life in a way that leads to their own satisfaction. Such individualism obstructs the revelation of a higher source of authority than one's self about the meaning and goal of human life. Judeo-Christian faith is entirely incompatible with today's individualism. The two dominant biblical images of the church—the people of God and the body of Christ—present Christianity as a community filled with the presence of the risen Lord and animated by the Holy Spirit. Christians cannot be isolated individuals, but are a community of disciples doing the work of justice and love as a tangible expression that the reign of God is upon us.

And a fifth cultural obstacle to God's word being implanted in the minds and hearts of individuals and society today is consumerism. Global capitalism has replaced the Roman Empire as the context in which the word of God must be proclaimed. The focal point of cities is no longer the cathedral spire topped with the cross, but the skyscraper topped with the corporate logo of its owner. Rampant consumerism has perverted human desires by redirecting them from their natural end in God to an artificial objective in material objects and temporary pleasures. In this environment, the ancient call to evangelize becomes distorted. Churches who want to increase their share of the market must ask themselves what will attract customers and meet their needs. What is called evangelization often looks more like church marketing. Offering multiple social choices and options for self-improvement becomes the first goal while less marketable aspects of Christian faith are removed.

Yet people eventually become discontent with our civilization of gadgets, entertainment, trends, and novelties, and they seek lasting meaning and purpose. In spite of all the obstacles of today's culture, we still profess with conviction that the gospel of Jesus Christ answers the truest needs and the deepest longings of the human heart. Today's challenge for the church is how to offer the authentic good news of God's reign to a world staggering under the weight of so many unanswered questions and unfulfilled longings.

Reflection and discussion

- What are some of the signs of these cultural obstacles in my own life today?

- What are some ways that communities of faith can help to overcome these five obstructions?

The Bible Communicates the Mission of God

All of Scripture witnesses to God's mission for the sake of the world. This mission springs from the reality that humanity has rebelled against God's original desire for creation and experiences the darkness of ignorance and despair. God's mission is to redeem the world, to restore the broken relationship, to bring light to the nations, and to bring about a new creation. It is a mission that embraces the whole of creation, time, and humanity within its scope. By inserting our own lives into the grand narrative of the Old and New Testaments, we unite our lives with God's mission, establishing within us a confident hope.

In order to fulfill the divine mission for the sake of the world, God calls forth Abraham and promises blessings to all the families of the earth through his descendants. The people of Israel become the bearers of God's mission for the world, as God makes them his own people and the instruments of his saving will on the earth. God desires to bless one people so that through them he can in turn bless all peoples. This is the message that Paul describes as the good news preached in advance, "the gospel beforehand" (Gal 3:8), the proclamation of God's overarching will, expressed throughout Scripture, to bring blessings to all the nations.

Through the Torah, prophets, and psalms, we come to know God and the kind of blessings he has in mind for the world. The whole of the Old Testament is oriented toward the future and impelled by hope. Through increasing revelation, manifested by the words and deeds of God among his people, we come to realize that, from the beginning to the end of God's mission, God desires to heal the world by calling it to ever-greater justice, beauty, goodness, and truth.

With the people of ancient Israel, we must look backward, forward, and outward. God's people must look backward to God's original intention for human life and forward to the end of time, to God's goal of a renewed humanity in a restored creation. And we must face outward to the nations, confronting idolatry, seeking justice, and embodying God's will so that all people might come to know and worship the true and living God. Facing outward as God's people, we join in his mission so that all people might experience his saving grace.

The word "evangelize," to declare good news, first occurs in the Old Testament in the context of Israel's imminent release from their exile and captivity in Babylon. Isaiah evokes the imagination and hope of his hearers with the image of a single messenger, an evangelizer running with the good news. Speeding across the mountains, he carries the news, announcing that God's promises are being fulfilled: "How beautiful upon the mountains are the feet of the messenger who announces peace, who brings good news, who announces salvation, who says to Zion, 'Your God reigns.' The Lord has bared his holy arm before the eyes of all the nations; and all the ends of the earth shall see the salvation of our God" (Isa 52:7, 10).

The good news that God returns, redeems, and reigns will ultimately benefit "all the nations." This good news spreads from a single messenger to "all the ends of the earth." The word of God opens outwardly from a word directed to Israel to a word with universal scope. God's word becomes good news for all people, a promise of salvation to the world.

But as the Old Testament period ends, Israel has failed in its mission to the nations. Languishing in the darkness, under the successive occupation of the Babylonian, Persian, Greek, and Roman empires, Israel longed for its Messiah, but was torn apart by factions—Pharisees, Sadducees, Zealots, and Essenes—each with a different vision of the coming kingdom and how God will bring it about. Each vision manifested a profound misunderstanding of God's purpose in choosing Israel. They developed attitudes of separatism from other peoples and affirmed their own privilege over other nations. Their history of being exploited manifested itself in bitter hatred for the Gentiles and a desire for vengeance toward the peoples of other nations.

The prophetic image of the coming kingdom of God looked nothing like the historical situation in which Israel found itself. By the time of Jesus, Israel was looking forward to a Messiah who would crush and destroy its Gentile enemies. The divided people hoped that God would punish the peoples of other nations—an expectation far different from God's desire to bring salvation to the ends of the earth.

In the New Testament, we see Israel's flame of hope blaze up from the earth's darkness and prepare the way for the dawn of God's kingdom. Israel's long-awaited Messiah will inaugurate an evangelizing mission that will bring the good news of God's salvation to the ends of the earth.

Reflection and discussion

- In what ways do the Scriptures call us to unite our lives with the mission of God?

- What are some reasons Israel was failing in its mission to be a light to the nations?

Reading the Bible as Missionary Disciples

The longer we live and the wiser we become, the more we realize that all of those things in which we are tempted to place our hopes—like material possessions, physical pleasures, and worldly power—are only temporary and fleeting. For Christian believers, what gives meaning to the world and purpose to life is the word of God. God has spoken his word in the history of salvation and definitively in the life, death, and resurrection of his Son. As

Peter addresses us in his first letter, "The word of the Lord endures forever. That word is the good news that was announced to you" (1 Peter 1:25).

Through the power and inspiration of the Holy Spirit, the Word of God became flesh, and the word of God became Scripture. This word of God has been entrusted to the church, which then hands it on through the apostles and its apostolic tradition. The mission of the church is to proclaim the word of God to the world. Because Scripture is God's self-revelation and divinely inspired, we hear, read, experience, and share it with others as the word of God. And as the word of God, Scripture forms us into missionary disciples.

The more each of us engages in a prayerful and faith-filled reading of the Bible and thereby deepens our relationship with Jesus Christ, the more we are able to participate in the church's mission of evangelization—proclaiming the word of God to the world. We cannot keep to ourselves the hope that is within us. Peter continues in his first letter, "Always be ready to make your defense to anyone who demands from you an accounting for the hope that is in you; yet do it with gentleness and reverence" (1 Peter 3:15–16).

We become missionary disciples by first being evangelized ourselves by the word of God. Through prayerful, faith-filled, reflective reading of Scripture, we become people who communicate the gospel to others by the witness of our lives. By becoming missionary disciples, we become ready to offer to others the reason for the hope that lies within us, the gospel that animates our lives. But, as Peter suggests, we must never use pressure or overwhelm others in our efforts to evangelize. Our motivation must always be love for others and a desire to help them remove whatever obstacles block the word of God from their lives. The work of missionary discipleship must always be done with gentleness, respect, reverence, and love.

The truest incentive for missionary discipleship comes from contemplating God's word with love, lingering over its pages, and reading it with the heart. Approached in this way, the beauty of Scripture will amaze and continually excite us. But if this is to come about, we need to listen to the word with a contemplative spirit, recognizing that we have been entrusted with a precious treasure that leads us to a new life. There is nothing more valuable that we can give to another.

Reflection and discussion

- Why is it important that we let ourselves be evangelized before we can bring the good news of Jesus Christ to others?

- What are some ways in which we can prepare ourselves to be missionary disciples?

Prayer

God of light, who has revealed yourself to the world and called your people to missionary discipleship, look upon me as I begin this study of your inspired word. Let your word so transform my mind and heart that I may respond more fully to your call to spread the good news of your Son, Jesus Christ. Send your Holy Spirit upon me to guide, encourage, and enlighten me as I contemplate the sacred texts of Scripture.

SUGGESTIONS FOR FACILITATORS, GROUP SESSION 1

1. If the group is meeting for the first time, or if there are newcomers joining the group, it is helpful to provide name tags.

2. Distribute the books to the members of the group.

3. You may want to ask the participants to introduce themselves and tell the group a bit about themselves.

4. Ask one or more of these introductory questions:
   - What drew you to join this group?
   - What is your biggest fear in beginning this Bible study?
   - How is beginning this study like a "threshold" for you?

5. You may want to pray this prayer as a group:
   Come upon us, Holy Spirit, to enlighten and guide us as we begin this study of missionary discipleship. You inspired the biblical authors to express your word as manifested to the people of Israel and most fully in the life of Jesus. Motivate us each day to read the Scriptures and deepen our understanding and love for these sacred texts. Bless us during this session and throughout the coming week with the fire of your love.

6. Read the Introduction aloud, pausing at each question for discussion. Group members may wish to write the insights of the group as each question is discussed. Encourage several members of the group to respond to each question.

7. Don't feel compelled to finish the complete Introduction during the session. It is better to allow sufficient time to talk about the questions raised than to rush to the end. Group members may read any remaining sections on their own after the group meeting.

8. Instruct group members to read the first six lessons on their own during the six days before the next group meeting. They should write out their own answers to the questions as preparation for next week's group discussion.

9. Fill in the date for each group meeting under "Schedule for Group Study."

10. Conclude by praying aloud together the prayer at the end of the Introduction.

He brought him outside and said, "Look toward heaven
and count the stars, if you are able to count them."
Then he said to him, "So shall your descendants be." GEN 15:5

Blessings to All the Peoples of the Earth

GENESIS 12:1–3 ¹*Now the Lord said to Abram, "Go from your country and your kindred and your father's house to the land that I will show you. ²I will make of you a great nation, and I will bless you, and make your name great, so that you will be a blessing. ³I will bless those who bless you, and the one who curses you I will curse; and in you all the families of the earth shall be blessed."*

GENESIS 15:1–5 ¹*After these things the word of the Lord came to Abram in a vision, "Do not be afraid, Abram, I am your shield; your reward shall be very great." ²But Abram said, "O Lord God, what will you give me, for I continue childless, and the heir of my house is Eliezer of Damascus?" ³And Abram said, "You have given me no offspring, and so a slave born in my house is to be my heir." ⁴But the word of the Lord came to him, "This man shall not be your heir; no one but your very own issue shall be your heir." ⁵He brought him outside and said, "Look toward heaven and count the stars, if you are able to count them." Then he said to him, "So shall your descendants be."*

According to Paul, the gospel begins in Genesis. There, in God's call to Abraham to go forth from his homeland and to be the bearer of God's mission, God begins a saving history that will extend to the whole world. God promises Abraham descendants as numerous as the stars of the sky, a land of their own, and most significantly, blessings through him for "all the families of the earth" (12:3). This is the message that Paul describes as the good news preached in advance, "the gospel beforehand" (Gal 3:8), the proclamation that God's overarching will throughout Scripture is to bring blessings to all the nations.

The Christian mission to the Gentiles, Paul taught, far from infidelity to God's covenant with Israel, was rather the fulfillment of it. This blessing for all the nations of the earth was the very purpose of Israel's existence in the broad plan of God. Since Jesus as Messiah embodies the identity and mission of Israel, then to belong to the Messiah through faith is to be a true child of Abraham. The ethnicity or national identity of the person no longer matters: "If you belong to Christ, then you are Abraham's offspring, heirs according to the promise" (Gal 3:29).

God's promise to Abraham, "In you all the nations of the earth shall be blessed," is a pivotal text for the whole Bible. It occurs five times in Genesis (12:3; 18:18; 22:18; 26:4; 28:14), the bottom line of God's covenant with Abraham. Despite a world filled with the darkness and ignorance that comes from rebellion against God's will (Gen 3–11), God's ultimate purpose is to bless humanity. A worldwide problem (human sin) requires a worldwide response. The story of how that universal blessing comes about occupies the rest of the Bible—Genesis 12 to Revelation 22. The call of Abraham forms the beginning of God's response to the maliciousness of human hearts, the conflict between nations, and the growing darkness that covers the earth. In Abraham and his barren wife, Sarah, God launches the world's redemption.

Before he could become God's vehicle of blessing to the whole earth, Abraham had to relinquish all that tied him to the land of Babylon: "your country and your kindred and your father's house" (12:1). The great Mesopotamian empires, centers of immense human pride, cannot solve humanity's deepest problems. God's mission requires a radical departure and a new start. The story of Babel's tower (Gen 11), a tale of human arrogance that results in global confusion, is met by Abraham's call with its promise of global blessings. God invests his blessings for all the earth in the fragile human vessel of an aging husband and a sterile wife. From them shall come descendants as numerous as the stars of heaven (15:5).

Abraham trusted in God's word and obeyed God's will. Likewise, those who are called to participate in this redemptive mission for the world must also exercise confident trust in God's promises and ready obedience to God's will. The promises of God to Abraham became the agenda for God's own mission to the nations, and the obedient response of Abraham became the model for our mission as God's people.

What Paul described as "the gospel beforehand" leads to the gospel of Jesus Christ. As the New Testament begins, Matthew initiates his gospel by affirming the Messiah as the son of Abraham, the fulfillment of the worldwide blessing God called Abraham to be. And Matthew concludes his gospel with the missionary mandate to make disciples of all nations, calling the church to complete the Abrahamic mission (Matt 1:1; 28:19).

Reflection and discussion

- Why was it necessary for Abraham to leave his homeland in order to initiate God's redeeming plan for the world?

- God tells Abraham, "Do not be afraid" (Gen 15:1). How has my faith developed through times of fear?

- In what ways is Abraham an ancient model for Christian discipleship?

- Why did Paul describe God's promises to Abraham as "the gospel beforehand" (Gal 3:8, 29)?

- When have I found it most difficult to trust in God? What can I do to begin trusting God more completely?

Prayer

Creator God, who made the whole world and all that fills it, you have entered into partnership with humanity to complete your design for creation. Bless us so that we may be a blessing for others, and help us to trust in your promises to redeem the world.

**"Surely this great nation is a wise and discerning people!"
For what other great nation has a god so near to it as the
Lord our God is whenever we call to him?** DEUT 4:6–7

A Priestly Kingdom
and a Holy Nation

EXODUS 19:3–6 ³*Then Moses went up to God; the Lord called to him from the mountain, saying, "Thus you shall say to the house of Jacob, and tell the Israelites: ⁴You have seen what I did to the Egyptians, and how I bore you on eagles' wings and brought you to myself. ⁵Now therefore, if you obey my voice and keep my covenant, you shall be my treasured possession out of all the peoples. Indeed, the whole earth is mine, ⁶but you shall be for me a priestly kingdom and a holy nation. These are the words that you shall speak to the Israelites."*

DEUTERONOMY 4:5–9 ⁵*See, just as the Lord my God has charged me, I now teach you statutes and ordinances for you to observe in the land that you are about to enter and occupy. ⁶You must observe them diligently, for this will show your wisdom and discernment to the peoples, who, when they hear all these statutes, will say, "Surely this great nation is a wise and discerning people!" ⁷For what other great nation has a god so near to it as the Lord our God is whenever we call to him? ⁸And what other great nation has statutes and ordinances as just as this entire law that I am setting before you today? ⁹But take care and watch yourselves closely, so as neither to forget the things that your eyes have seen nor to let them slip from your mind all the days of your life; make them known to your children and your children's children.*

T he account of the exodus from Egypt extends the narrative of Abraham's family to the formation of the nation of Israel. Through God's choice of this particular people, God wishes to unfold his universal blessings. Through the history of Israel, God wants to show the other nations the beginnings of the sort of world he intends to bring about through his saving work. So God's singular people and their history have been chosen for the sake of God's mission and for the sake of others toward whom God's mission is directed.

As slaves in Egypt, God's people were living under Pharaoh, caught up in his dictatorial rule and his idolatrous system. When God sees them living in such harsh conditions, he acts to rescue them. God calls Moses to be his instrument with Pharaoh, and God delivers his people from bondage with signs and wonders so that the Egyptians will know that God is the Lord. Leading his people into the wilderness, God forms a solemn and binding covenant with them. On Mount Sinai, God tells his people why he, the Lord of all nations, has chosen to liberate one nation and bind them to himself in covenant. Even though the whole earth belongs to God, Israel belongs to God in a special sense and has been chosen for a special task (Exod 19:5–6). God's choice of Israel is not an end in itself but is the means to a much greater end.

Israel is chosen to be "a priestly kingdom." What priests are for God's people, Israel is for the world of nations. In the Old Testament, priests are set apart by God to mediate God's presence and blessings to others. Thus, Israel is called to be a tangible indication of God's presence to the surrounding nations and to bring God's blessings to all the other peoples. In addition, Israel is chosen to be "a holy nation." Holiness is the quality of something that has been set apart and consecrated to God's service. So Israel has been removed from the other nations and dedicated to God's mission for the world. Throughout the remainder of the Torah, God teaches his people how their lives are to be markedly different from those of the peoples around them. Israel must showcase to the world what it means to be a people in covenant with God.

God has freed his people and brought them into covenant in order to carry out his redeeming mission in the world. They are made a priestly and holy people for the sake of the nations, but they will not bring God's blessings and saving presence to others through their own strength. God will be among his people, acting in wonderful deeds to make himself known to the peoples of the earth. God first acts *in* his people, then God works *through* his people for the sake of the world.

Before Israel enters into the land God has promised, Moses exhorts the people to observe the Torah so that they will have abundant life and so that they will be a witness to the nations around them (Deut 4:6). Israel will live out its history under the constant surveillance of the ancient world. Israel's land is at the crossroads of the nations so that God's people may be seen by the other peoples. Moses urges them to be faithful to the covenant and to follow God's decrees. In this way, the peoples of the world will see their wisdom and know that God is near to them.

In addition to fidelity to the Torah, another critical task of Israel in their role as witnesses is the responsibility of instructing the next generation. Moses urges the people to remember and teach their children (Deut 4:9–10). The people are in constant danger of forgetting God's saving deeds and the way of life God set forth for them. To the surrounding nations and to the next generation, God's people must be a model for what God has done and continues to do.

Reflection and discussion

- What is Israel's role as "a priestly kingdom and a holy nation" in the context of their covenant with God?

- How does God's covenant language to Israel in Exodus compare to God's covenant language to Abraham in Genesis?

- In what ways does God want Israel to be a witness and showcase to the world?

- How does the experience of Israel teach us that we must first be evangelized ourselves before we can evangelize others?

Prayer

Redeeming God, who led your people out of bondage into freedom so they could be a witness to your presence, help me to model for others what it means to be in covenant with you. Make me a witness to your liberating power and redeeming love.

"Hear in heaven your dwelling place, and do according to all that the foreigner calls to you, so that all the peoples of the earth may know your name and fear you, as do your people Israel." 1 KINGS 8:43

May His Glory Fill the Whole Earth

2 SAMUEL 7:12–17 *¹²When your days are fulfilled and you lie down with your ancestors, I will raise up your offspring after you, who shall come forth from your body, and I will establish his kingdom. ¹³He shall build a house for my name, and I will establish the throne of his kingdom forever. ¹⁴I will be a father to him, and he shall be a son to me. When he commits iniquity, I will punish him with a rod such as mortals use, with blows inflicted by human beings. ¹⁵But I will not take my steadfast love from him, as I took it from Saul, whom I put away from before you. ¹⁶Your house and your kingdom shall be made sure forever before me; your throne shall be established forever. ¹⁷In accordance with all these words and with all this vision, Nathan spoke to David.*

1 KINGS 8:41–43 *⁴¹"Likewise when a foreigner, who is not of your people Israel, comes from a distant land because of your name ⁴²—for they shall hear of your great name, your mighty hand, and your outstretched arm—when a foreigner comes and prays toward this house, ⁴³then hear in heaven your dwelling place, and do according to all that the foreigner calls to you, so that all the peoples of the earth may know your name and fear you, as do your people Israel, and so that they may know that your name has been invoked on this house that I have built."*

PSALM 72:17–19

[17]*May his name endure forever,*
his fame continue as long as the sun.
May all nations be blessed in him;
may they pronounce him happy.
[18]*Blessed be the Lord, the God of Israel,*
who alone does wondrous things.
[19]*Blessed be his glorious name forever;*
may his glory fill the whole earth. Amen and Amen.

Following the call of Abraham and the exodus of Moses, another era of Israel's saga is characterized by kings with royal courts and priests with a wondrous temple. The books of Samuel and Kings describe the monarchy in the line of David and the temple in Jerusalem. These blessings of God are designed to support Israel in its calling to be a holy and priestly nation in witness to the surrounding peoples. David provides a model for what a king for Israel should be. He mediates God's rule, since God is Israel's true king. He removes the threat of idolatry by defeating Israel's enemies, he promotes worship and sacrifice in Jerusalem, and he administers the Torah with justice for the poor and weak so that Israel becomes again an exemplar for the surrounding nations.

Because David submitted the life of the nation to God's rule, God offers hope for the future through him. In making a covenant with the king, God promises that one of David's descendants will rule over a universal and ever-lasting kingdom (2 Sam 7:16; Ps 2:7–8). God's covenant with David and his royal house fits within the worldwide vision of God's covenant with Abraham. The reign of David in Jerusalem becomes the prototype for the reign of God that will bring the restoration of all that God desires for human-ity within creation.

The author of Psalm 72 prays that the promise made to Abraham may be fulfilled in Israel's future king: "May all nations be blessed in him" (Ps 72:17). Through the reign of this ideal king in the line of David, Israel will fulfill its calling to bring God's blessings to the peoples of all nations. As Matthew's gospel announces, Jesus is the Messiah, "the son of David, the son of Abraham." Embodying both the Abrahamic and Davidic promises, he is the one who will pass on the task of missionary discipleship to Abraham's spiritual heirs.

The temple in Jerusalem, built by Solomon, the son of David, brings hope that God's glorious presence and Israel's worship will serve as witness to the world. At the dedication of the temple, Solomon prays that God will not only hear the people of Israel when they pray, but also that God will hear foreigners from distant lands who are drawn to the temple to know and serve God (1 Kings 8:41–43). The king prays that when God hears the prayers of the foreigners, "all the peoples of the earth" may know and invoke God's name. Isaiah envisions the day when God's temple in Jerusalem will be a place of worship and sacrifice for people of all nations and will be called "a house of prayer for all peoples" (Isa 56:6–7).

These texts share the same universal vision as the call of Abraham in Genesis. Just as God chose one person to be the vessel of blessings to the nations, God chooses one place, the royal temple in Jerusalem, as the focal point for God's blessings to all the peoples of the earth. God's future Messiah will be descended from the "house of David," from David's royal line, and will be the "house of God," the new place of God's dwelling upon the earth. That which seems the most particular focus of the life of Israel, the monarchy and the temple, will become the sources of God's universal grace.

Reflection and discussion

- In what ways does God's covenant with David emphasize the worldwide scope of God's promised future?

- Psalm 72 is regarded in Jewish and Christian tradition as a messianic psalm. In what ways does it reiterate God's worldwide mission to the nations?

- How do the monarchy of David and the temple in Jerusalem promote the call of Israel to be "a priestly kingdom and a holy nation"?

- How do God's covenants with Abraham, Moses, and David form the essential foundation for my call to missionary discipleship?

Prayer

Universal Lord, who promised blessings to all nations, you have formed your covenant through Abraham, Moses, and David. Help me to imitate their confident trust in your promises so that I may be a witness to your reign over the world, now and into the future.

Let the peoples praise you, O God; let all the
peoples praise you. Let the nations be glad and sing for joy,
for you judge the peoples with equity and guide the
nations upon earth. PSALM 67:3–4

All the Ends of the Earth
Will Worship the Lord

PSALM 22:27–31

27 *All the ends of the earth shall remember*
    and turn to the Lord;
and all the families of the nations
    shall worship before him.
28 *For dominion belongs to the Lord,*
    and he rules over the nations.
29 *To him, indeed, shall all who sleep in the earth bow down;*
    before him shall bow all who go down to the dust,
    and I shall live for him.
30 *Posterity will serve him;*
    future generations will be told about the Lord,
31 *and proclaim his deliverance to a people yet unborn,*
    saying that he has done it.

PSALM 67:1–7

¹*May God be gracious to us and bless us*
    and make his face to shine upon us,
²*that your way may be known upon earth,*
    your saving power among all nations.
³*Let the peoples praise you, O God;*
    let all the peoples praise you.
⁴*Let the nations be glad and sing for joy,*
    for you judge the peoples with equity
    and guide the nations upon earth.
⁵*Let the peoples praise you, O God;*
    let all the peoples praise you.
⁶*The earth has yielded its increase;*
    God, our God, has blessed us.
⁷*May God continue to bless us;*
    let all the ends of the earth revere him.

PSALM 102:18–22

¹⁸*Let this be recorded for a generation to come,*
    so that a people yet unborn may praise the Lord:
¹⁹*that he looked down from his holy height,*
    from heaven the Lord looked at the earth,
²⁰*to hear the groans of the prisoners,*
    to set free those who were doomed to die;
²¹*so that the name of the Lord may be declared in Zion,*
    and his praise in Jerusalem,
²²*when peoples gather together,*
    and kingdoms, to worship the Lord.

The hymnbook of the temple, the Book of Psalms, nourishes the prayer of God's people and highlights their mission to the world. The psalms express their fears and hopes, sadness and joy, memories of the past and visions of the future. These traditional prayers, which God's people sung both in their hearts and in public worship, became the prayers of Jesus and his disciples, and thus the prayers of the church.

In many of the psalms, the personal concerns of the singer broaden out to encompass a much wider scope. In Psalm 22, the intense suffering of the worshiper expressed in the opening verse, "My God my God, why have you forsaken me" (Ps 22:1), leads to a range of trust that encompasses "all the ends of the earth," "all the families of the nations," "all who sleep in the earth," and "a people yet unborn." Jesus found in this psalm not only the words that described his own suffering, but the assurance that his death would not be in vain. Through his death and resurrection, God would open the way for the universal worship of all the nations, including those who have died and those not yet born.

Psalm 67 asks that God bless his people, not only for their own sake, but with the hope that it result in international acclaim for God. The first two verses introduce the theme, combining a prayer for God's blessing upon Israel with the request that God's ways may be known among all the nations of the earth. The worshipers' reason for seeking God's blessing is not self-centered but serves the wider purpose of revealing God's salvation throughout the world. Verses 3 and 5 form a refrain, invoking God's praise among all people, and verse 4 forms the center of the psalm and its longest verse. God's judgment is a cause for joy because God treats all peoples with fairness (67:4).

The final two verses underscore the ultimate purpose of God's blessings upon his people: "let all the ends of the earth revere him" (67:7). What draws the other nations of the world to give reverence to God is not military subjugation or annexation to Israel, but blessings upon God's own people. The goal is not the extension of Israel's kingdom but the extension of God's praise. God chose Israel as his own holy and priestly people as his means of spreading blessings to all people. God's ultimate aim is to publicize his saving ways to the whole world.

Psalm 102 invokes praise of God for his liberating compassion. Although God looks upon the whole earth from his heavenly perspective, he listens to "the groans of the prisoners" and sets free "those who are doomed to die" (102:19–20). God's glory is manifested not as royal spectacle but as attention to the destitute. This evokes praise of God in Zion, an acclaim that will extend to future generations (102:18) and to the peoples of other nations, who will assemble to worship the Lord (102:22).

The temple and its hymnbook draw in God's people to worship, and then they direct them outward to witness to all. In word, worship, and witness, God's people express their universal vision and the ultimate goal of God's saving work among them. All of these psalms reiterate the message that whatever God does for Israel is ultimately for the benefit of the whole world. The psalms promise a future in which the nations will join Israel in worshiping God. The Israelites are the channel of God's blessings for all people. Through them, God will extend his blessings to all.

Reflection and discussion

- How do these psalms help me to broaden the scope of my prayer? How might this hymnbook of Israel become the book of prayer for missionary disciples?

- What further meaning can I grasp in these psalms when I read them through the eyes, mind, and heart of Jesus?

Prayer

Merciful Lord, who rules the whole world yet looks with compassion on those most in need, let all the peoples praise you. Direct our vision outward, beyond our own needs and desires, so that we may see as you see, feel as you feel, and act as you act.

**Turn to me and be saved, all the ends of the earth!
For I am God, and there is no other.** ISA 45:22

I Will Give You as a Light to the Nations

ISAIAH 42:5–9

⁵*Thus says God, the Lord,*
> *who created the heavens and stretched them out,*
> *who spread out the earth and what comes from it,*
who gives breath to the people upon it
> *and spirit to those who walk in it:*
⁶*I am the Lord, I have called you in righteousness,*
> *I have taken you by the hand and kept you;*
I have given you as a covenant to the people,
> *a light to the nations,*
⁷*to open the eyes that are blind,*
to bring out the prisoners from the dungeon,
> *from the prison those who sit in darkness.*
⁸*I am the Lord, that is my name;*
> *my glory I give to no other,*
> *nor my praise to idols.*
⁹*See, the former things have come to pass,*
> *and new things I now declare;*
before they spring forth,
> *I tell you of them.*

ISAIAH 45:22–23

²²*Turn to me and be saved,*
all the ends of the earth!
For I am God, and there is no other.
²³*By myself I have sworn,*
from my mouth has gone forth in righteousness
a word that shall not return:
"To me every knee shall bow,
every tongue shall swear."

ISAIAH 49:6–7

⁶*[The Lord] says,*
"It is too light a thing that you should be my servant
to raise up the tribes of Jacob
and to restore the survivors of Israel;
I will give you as a light to the nations,
that my salvation may reach to the end of the earth."
⁷*Thus says the Lord,*
the Redeemer of Israel and his Holy One,
to one deeply despised, abhorred by the nations,
the slave of rulers,
"Kings shall see and stand up,
princes, and they shall prostrate themselves,
because of the Lord, who is faithful,
the Holy One of Israel, who has chosen you."

The prophets challenge the Israelites when they forget their identity, break the covenant, and obscure their witness to the peoples of the earth. When God's people highlight only their own privilege, seek their own security, and take for granted the salvation they receive from God, the prophets admonish them with threats of destruction and persuade them to remember their outward-facing mission. In every period of its history, Israel needs its prophets to renew their identity and direct them toward their missionary responsibility to other nations.

Israel's outward mission to the world is particularly expressed in the prophecies of the Lord's Servant in Isaiah. This Servant is both the Messiah and a collective term for the ideal Israel. The speaker addressing the Servant is the Lord, the creator of the heavens and the earth, who cares for the cosmos and its inhabitants (42:5). God is close to his Servant, charging him to do God's own work in the world. Through this messianic figure, Israel will bring blessings to all the nations, as God promised to Abraham. Through the obedience of the Lord's Servant, without spectacle or apparent power, God will rule over the earth.

The Lord charges his Servant to be "a covenant to the people, a light to the nations" (42:6). God wants to fashion a people whose very existence in the world is a living testimony to his rule over the world. Every aspect of Israel's existence—domestic, social, economic, and political—was to reflect God's character as creator and liberator. These parallel terms—covenant to the people and light to the nations—express the universal dimension of the task God gives to his Servant. The witness of the Servant will be the means of drawing all people into the covenant relationship with God. This covenant, of which Israel has already been a part, is now to be extended to the wider family of the nations.

This witness will be a "light" by which the nations of the earth will share in God's salvation (42:7). The metaphor emphasizes the liberation of "those who sit in darkness," both the individual darkness of spiritual blindness and the communal imprisonment in the dungeon. The creator of the world will bring about a new creation for the whole world. The one who liberated Israel from bondage will bring liberating salvation for all the people of the earth. God wants to open blind eyes and break into the dungeon with the light of divine revelation.

God's mission for his Servant is stated more explicitly: "I will give you as a light to the nations, that my salvation may reach to the end of the earth" (49:6). Restoring the twelve tribes of Israel is not a large-enough task. This astonishing call—to save the world—is more than any prophet or any nation can do. It is clearly the work of God, the One who is "the Lord, the Redeemer of Israel and his Holy One" (49:7). The description of the Servant expresses his lowliness: "one deeply despised, abhorred by the nations, the slave of rulers." To this Servant, who is worthless and rejected, the rulers of the world will stand in awed respect and bow in homage.

Between these two Servant passages, Isaiah proclaims the word of the Lord, urging all the peoples of the earth to turn to the only God to be saved (Isa 45:22). Salvation is not reserved only to Israel, whose God is the Lord. If God is the only God of the whole earth and his desire is to save, then he is the only Savior of the whole world as well. The "word" of God goes forth from the "mouth" of God and does not "return" (45:23); rather, it accomplishes its aim of announcing salvation to "all the ends of the earth."

The New Testament shows that these Servant prophecies are fulfilled completely in Jesus the Messiah. Paul and Barnabas explain their missionary task by quoting these words from Isaiah: "I have set you to be a light for the Gentiles, so that you may bring salvation to the ends of the earth" (Acts 13:47). In his beautiful hymn to Christ's humility, Paul uses Isaiah's words to proclaim that Jesus will be exalted over all. At his name, "every knee should bend" throughout the cosmos, and "every tongue should confess" that he is Lord (Phil 2:10–11).

Reflection and discussion

- In what sense is the mission of God's Servant a model for missionary discipleship?

- In what ways can a study of God's call to his servant in Isaiah help disciples of Jesus better understand their mission as "the light of the world" (Matt 5:14)?

Prayer

Redeemer and Holy One of Israel, you have called your people to be a light to the nations, bringing your salvation to the ends of the earth. Give me the grace to illumine the darkened lives of others so that they may know that you are the Lord to whom every knee should bow and every tongue confess.

**Their burnt offerings and their sacrifices will be accepted on my altar;
for my house shall be called a house of prayer for all peoples.**

ISA 56:7

God Will Offer Salvation to the Outcasts

ISAIAH 56:1–8

¹*Thus says the Lord:*
Maintain justice, and do what is right,
for soon my salvation will come,
     and my deliverance be revealed.
²*Happy is the mortal who does this,*
     the one who holds it fast,
who keeps the sabbath, not profaning it,
     and refrains from doing any evil.

³*Do not let the foreigner joined to the Lord say,*
     "The Lord will surely separate me from his people";
and do not let the eunuch say,
     "I am just a dry tree."
⁴*For thus says the Lord:*
To the eunuchs who keep my sabbaths,
     who choose the things that please me
     and hold fast my covenant,

⁵*I will give, in my house and within my walls,*
  a monument and a name
  better than sons and daughters;
I will give them an everlasting name
  that shall not be cut off.

⁶*And the foreigners who join themselves to the Lord,*
  to minister to him, to love the name of the Lord,
  and to be his servants,
all who keep the sabbath, and do not profane it,
  and hold fast my covenant—
⁷*these I will bring to my holy mountain,*
  and make them joyful in my house of prayer;
their burnt offerings and their sacrifices
  will be accepted on my altar;
for my house shall be called a house of prayer
  for all peoples.
⁸*Thus says the Lord God,*
  who gathers the outcasts of Israel,
I will gather others to them
  besides those already gathered.

The prophets speak against two temptations that would cause Israel to lose its divine mission. The first danger is isolation. Withdrawing from the other nations could protect the Israelites' own beliefs and practices, but they would fail to be the showcase to the other peoples of the world that God expected them to be. The second danger is assimilation. Identifying themselves with the other nations and assimilating their culture would cause Israel to lose its distinctive identity and dilute its covenant with God. To avoid these two dangers, Israel developed structures of leadership, institutions of worship, and its sacred literature to maintain its unique identity and witness among the foreign empires. In the midst of the overwhelming imperial cultures in which the Israelites live, they must bear in mind their unique God-given identity, the covenanted community to which they belong, and the one God of all the nations whom they serve. They must remember their unique calling to be a blessing to all the nations and to await the fulfillment of God's purposes with hope.

Here Isaiah presents God's vision for an open but faithful community, a community open to outsiders but requiring that they maintain the distinctiveness of God's covenant. The covenant stipulations are primarily a matter of an authentic relationship with the one God of Israel. Maintaining this living relationship with God by those who "maintain justice and do what is right" issues forth into the experience of God's salvation and deliverance (verse 1).

Isaiah's references to foreigners and eunuchs would have been shocking to those insisting on Israel's isolation from other peoples in order to maintain its distinctive way of life (verse 3). For the Torah explicitly excluded eunuchs, Ammonites, and Moabites from the assembly of the Lord (Deut 23:1–3). But Isaiah specifically states that these outcasts must be welcomed in Israel's congregation, provided they keep the Sabbath and hold fast to the covenant.

This prophetic message expresses the limitless grace of God. The foreigners and eunuchs are told not to denigrate themselves. They are not cast out and worthless; they are people of dignity and value. Although the eunuchs are unable to have children to carry on their name after death, God will give them "a monument and a name" (*yad vashem*, in Hebrew) within God's house. They will, in fact, share in God's eternity and never be cut off (verse 5). Although the foreigners do not share the bloodline of Abraham, God will treat them just as he would any believing Israelite. God will welcome them in Jerusalem, and they will offer sacrifice at God's altar (verse 7).

The oracle of God teaches that it is not those who share the lineage of Abraham and pass it on to their offspring who are especially pleasing to God. Rather, God's people are those who manifest a living relationship with the God of all the earth. Even though they never knew Abraham and died childless, they are truly God's children. God desires those who love what he loves, hate what he hates, and want what he wants. If anyone lives this way, their ancestry, their body, and their abilities have nothing to do with their acceptability before God.

God said, "My house shall be called a house of prayer for all peoples" (verse 7). This is what Solomon foresaw at the temple's dedication long before (1 Kings 8:41–43). God chose Israel for his covenant not to shut out the world but to bring in the world. God's segregation of the Israelites from the world was never for the purpose of keeping God and his blessings for themselves. Rather, their separation was only to prevent Israel from being absorbed into the world, thus losing the ability to call the world into the blessings God promised through Abraham to all the nations. Indeed, Luke must have had this passage in mind when recounting in Acts the conversion of the Ethiopian official, the first believer in Jesus from outside the Jewish community. This man was a foreigner and a eunuch, and he was reading the scroll of Isaiah (Acts 8:26–40). This missionary discipleship demonstrates that faith in Jesus brings joy, blessings, and salvation to the outcasts of all nations.

Reflection and discussion

- Isaiah's oracle specifies the foreigners and eunuchs as examples of those seen as outcasts from God's assembly? Who are the outcasts of today who must receive acceptance from God's people?

- How are the opposite temptations of isolation and assimilation still dangers for people joined to God in covenant?

Prayer

God of merciful compassion, who welcomes the outcasts, you give all people an everlasting name and welcome them at your holy altar. Help me to welcome the outsiders and embrace them among the community of disciples.

SUGGESTIONS FOR FACILITATORS, GROUP SESSION 2

1. If there are newcomers who were not present for the first group session, introduce them now.

2. You may want to pray this prayer as a group:
   Faithful God, who formed your covenant with the descendants of Abraham and called them to carry your blessings to all peoples, summon us to be a light to the nations and to witness your reign in all the world. Help us demonstrate an open heart to the outcasts and a guiding hand to those who are lost. As we study these ancient Scriptures, continue to form our lives so that we may love what you love and do what you desire.

3. Ask one or more of the following questions:
   - What was your biggest challenge in Bible study over this past week?
   - What did you learn about God's love from your study this week?
   - What did you learn about yourself this week?

4. Discuss lessons 1 through 6 together. Assuming that group members have read the Scripture and commentary during the week, there is no need to read it aloud. As you review each lesson, you might want to briefly summarize the Scripture passages of each lesson and ask the group what stands out most clearly from the commentary.

5. Choose one or more of the questions for reflection and discussion from each lesson to talk over as a group. You may want to ask the group which question was most challenging or helpful to them as you review each lesson.

6. Keep the discussion moving, but don't rush in order to complete more questions. Allow time for the questions that provoke the most discussion.

7. Instruct group members to complete lessons 7 through 12 on their own before the next group meeting. They should write out their own answers to the questions as preparation for next week's group discussion.

8. Conclude by praying aloud together the prayer at the end of lesson 6, or any other prayer you choose.

[Jesus] said to them, "Follow me, and I will make you fish for people."
Immediately they left their nets and followed him.

MATT 4:19–20

The Call to Missionary Discipleship

MATTHEW 4:12–25 [12]*Now when Jesus heard that John had been arrested, he withdrew to Galilee.* [13]*He left Nazareth and made his home in Capernaum by the sea, in the territory of Zebulun and Naphtali,* [14]*so that what had been spoken through the prophet Isaiah might be fulfilled:*

[15]*"Land of Zebulun, land of Naphtali,*
 on the road by the sea, across the Jordan, Galilee of the Gentiles—
[16]*the people who sat in darkness*
 have seen a great light,
and for those who sat in the region and shadow of death
 light has dawned."

[17]*From that time Jesus began to proclaim, "Repent, for the kingdom of heaven has come near."*

[18]*As he walked by the Sea of Galilee, he saw two brothers, Simon, who is called Peter, and Andrew his brother, casting a net into the sea—for they were fishermen.* [19]*And he said to them, "Follow me, and I will make you fish for people."* [20]*Immediately they left their nets and followed him.* [21]*As he went from there, he saw two other brothers, James son of Zebedee and his brother John, in the boat with their father Zebedee, mending their nets, and he called them.* [22]*Immediately they left the boat and their father, and followed him.*

²³*Jesus went throughout Galilee, teaching in their synagogues and proclaiming the good news of the kingdom and curing every disease and every sickness among the people.* ²⁴*So his fame spread throughout all Syria, and they brought to him all the sick, those who were afflicted with various diseases and pains, demoniacs, epileptics, and paralytics, and he cured them.* ²⁵*And great crowds followed him from Galilee, the Decapolis, Jerusalem, Judea, and from beyond the Jordan.*

During the time of ancient Israel, God's people were called to be witnesses to the peoples around them, to be a light to the nations through commitment to their covenant relationship with God. By working within the history of Israel, God wanted to show the other nations the beginnings of the salvation he intends to bring to the world. As a holy and priestly nation, Israel was to face outward and witness the one true God to other peoples, yet they were given no mandate to go out to the nations as missionaries. But with the coming of Jesus as Israel's Messiah, God brought his own kingdom to Israel in Jesus, who brought God's promises and Israel's hopes to fulfillment. As Jesus restored Israel to its calling—to be a light to the nations and the channel of God's blessings—he formed the nucleus of his church. And in so doing, Jesus transformed the missionary vision of God's people into the energetic practice of evangelization.

Jesus begins his ministry in the fishing region of Galilee, evoking the gospel writer to cite the prophetic text of Isaiah. Into this place, waiting "in darkness" and in the "shadow of death," Jesus brings the "light" of the kingdom of God (verse 16). In him, God has come near his people and God's reign is immediately experienced. Jesus declares, "Repent, for the kingdom of heaven has come near" (verse 17). Although Jesus never clearly defines what he means by "kingdom," his hearers know from the ancient Scriptures that it is the restoration of God's reign over all creation. In Jesus, God's kingdom is imminent. Israel's hope has become reality. The arrival of God's kingdom means that God is dynamically establishing his rule. God is activating his saving power in Jesus through the Holy Spirit. Jesus is defeating the reign of evil in the world, reversing its consequences: physical and mental disease, demonic possession, shame and guilt, food scarcity, self-righteousness, exploitation of the poor, and even the chaotic forces of nature.

The first disciples Jesus calls to share his mission are simple fishermen, not the religious elite whom one might expect for a such a mission. His invitation is simple: "Follow me" (verse 19). The fishermen abandon their nets but they will still be fishing, casting a different kind of net through their own missionary discipleship.

What the people of Israel hoped God would do in the last days is now being done in the ministry of Jesus. In him, the last days are irrupting into the present. The evangelization of Jesus is accomplished not just with words announcing God's kingdom but with accompanying deeds (verses 23–24). In this way, the whole of his life and ministry may be considered a gospel proclamation, the announcement that God reigns over the earth.

The kingdom to which Jesus invites his listeners is not a different or distant world. Nor is the missionary discipleship to which he calls the fishermen a temporary or personal challenge. Rather, Jesus invites his followers into a community of disciples, a new gathering demanding an altered set of allegiances. He invites them to enter God's kingdom, which relativizes one's family relationships and national identities, and which challenges the status quo regarding the poor, tax collectors, lepers, prostitutes, Samaritans, and those normally excluded. And it is through this new family of God, embodying the practices and disciplines that manifest God's reign, that God's kingdom is offered to the world.

Reflection and discussion

- In what ways is coming to know Jesus like moving from darkness to light?

- How does the acceptance of Jesus' call by the fishermen compare to my response to the call of Jesus?

- What kinds of changes are necessary in the lives of those who accept Jesus' call to missionary discipleship?

- In what sense is my missionary discipleship an announcement of the presence of God's reign in the world today?

Prayer

Lord Jesus, you walked the shores of the Sea of Galilee and invited people to follow you. Come into my life today, call me by name, and give me a mission to serve your kingdom.

"Let your light shine before others, so that they may see your good works and give glory to your Father in heaven." MATT 5:16

Salt and Light for the World

MATTHEW 5:1–16 ¹*When Jesus saw the crowds, he went up the mountain; and after he sat down, his disciples came to him.* ²*Then he began to speak, and taught them, saying:*
³*"Blessed are the poor in spirit, for theirs is the kingdom of heaven.*
⁴*"Blessed are those who mourn, for they will be comforted.*
⁵*"Blessed are the meek, for they will inherit the earth.*
⁶*"Blessed are those who hunger and thirst for righteousness, for they will be filled.*
⁷*"Blessed are the merciful, for they will receive mercy.*
⁸*"Blessed are the pure in heart, for they will see God.*
⁹*"Blessed are the peacemakers, for they will be called children of God.*
¹⁰*"Blessed are those who are persecuted for righteousness' sake, for theirs is the kingdom of heaven.*
¹¹*"Blessed are you when people revile you and persecute you and utter all kinds of evil against you falsely on my account.* ¹²*Rejoice and be glad, for your reward is great in heaven, for in the same way they persecuted the prophets who were before you.*
¹³*"You are the salt of the earth; but if salt has lost its taste, how can its saltiness be restored? It is no longer good for anything, but is thrown out and trampled under foot.*
¹⁴*"You are the light of the world. A city built on a hill cannot be hid.* ¹⁵*No one after lighting a lamp puts it under the bushel basket, but on the lampstand, and it gives light to all in the house.*¹⁶*In the same way, let your light shine before others, so that they may see your good works and give glory to your Father in heaven."*

Having proclaimed that the kingdom of heaven has come near, Jesus begins to teach what life is like under the reign of God. Although this Sermon on the Mount is addressed immediately to the crowd that has gathered at the mountain, these teachings of Jesus are addressed to God's people of all times, and they describe the way of life for his disciples.

The eight beatitudes name the chief character traits of those who are "blessed" by God. These eight characteristics are evidence of God's gracious gifts offered to those who reform their lives at the message of God's kingdom. These beatitudes are divided into two sets of four: first, those qualities that describe a disciple's relationship with God (verses 3–6), then, those qualities that describe a disciple's relationship with other people (verses 7–10). Each of these eight characteristics of blessedness is followed by a promise of God. The present experience of God's reign in Jesus motivates the disciple to live in hopeful confidence of its future intensification.

These eight character traits must be cultivated during the lifelong process of discipleship so that they become more dynamically present in the life of each disciple. The "poor in spirit" are those who admit their poverty and acknowledge their total dependence on God. Those who cultivate this trust in God will begin experiencing the kingdom in their present lives as they await its full realization. "Those who mourn" are those who lament their own sins as well as the sin of the world. The mourning that results from afflictions and persecution will be met with God's future comfort. The "meek" are those who possess an unassuming humility, based on the model of Jesus. These meek ones—rather than those stocked with wealth, status, and arms—will ultimately inherit the earth. "Those who hunger and thirst for righteousness" realize their lack of right behavior before God and desire that faithful living permeate society and culture. This deep desire for God's will to be done on earth will be satisfied with the full coming of God's kingdom.

The second set of beatitudes, describing a disciple's qualities in relationship to other people, begins with the divine attribute of mercy. Those who are "merciful" in relationship to other people demonstrate compassion and loving kindness modeled on the life and teachings of Jesus. Those who deal mercifully with others will receive God's ultimate mercy and obtain the promises of his faithful love. Those who are "pure in heart" possess an internal integrity that manifests itself in both their private and public lives. Their single-hearted devotion to God's will results in seeing God, something that is impossible in this life but is part of the blessings of the world to come. The "peacemakers" are those who actively seek harmonious relationships with others. Their experience of peace with God enables them to strive for the cessation of hostilities and active reconciliation between people, while awaiting God's ultimate peace to come upon the world. Persecution "for righteousness' sake" is what those seeking to live the values taught by Jesus can expect to experience, but the second assurance of "the kingdom of heaven" brings the beatitudes full circle (verses 3, 10).

The lives of those living under God's reign are marked by humility toward God and mercy toward others. Though we might expect such humble, merciful people to be valued by other people, such is not the case for most disciples of Jesus. Scorn, insult, and abuse are what followers of Jesus more often receive in the present age (verses 11–12). Though this assurance of blessedness might seem to be an additional beatitude, it is more of an expansion of the others. Those who receive harassment and maltreatment must not simply endure it but experience it with deep joy, knowing that they are following in the way of the prophets before them and identifying themselves with Jesus, who was persecuted to the point of death. These countercultural blessings of the beatitudes mark Christian disciples as out of step with the world and as witnesses to God's kingdom.

As missionary disciples bear witness by living out the beatitudes, they become "the salt of the earth" and "the light of the world" (verses 13–16). Their mission has a wide horizon, far beyond the narrow circle of the disciples themselves. Like salt, they bring zest to the world and bring out the best in others. As light in the world, they are a flame of faith and a beacon of hope. Without visible works, a disciple is of no more value than tasteless salt or a lamp under a basket. Authentic disciples affect people through the character traits named in the beatitudes, and as people see their good works, they give glory to God.

Reflection and discussion

- What are the opposites of each of these eight qualities of discipleship? In other words, what eight characteristics must missionary disciples avoid?

- How are the beatitudes related to Jesus' words about salt and light?

- How can I be like salt and light so that I am a clearer witness of Jesus for others?

Prayer

Divine Teacher, you guide your disciples to understand the ways of God's kingdom, and you bring blessings into the lives of those who follow you. Transform me into the kind of person described by the beatitudes so that I may be a clearer witness to you.

Jesus came and said to them, "All authority in heaven and on earth has been given to me. Go therefore and make disciples of all nations."

MATT 28:18–19

Commissioning the Disciples to Evangelize

MATTHEW 28:16–20 ¹⁶*Now the eleven disciples went to Galilee, to the mountain to which Jesus had directed them.* ¹⁷*When they saw him, they worshiped him; but some doubted.* ¹⁸*And Jesus came and said to them, "All authority in heaven and on earth has been given to me.* ¹⁹*Go therefore and make disciples of all nations, baptizing them in the name of the Father and of the Son and of the Holy Spirit,* ²⁰*and teaching them to obey everything that I have commanded you. And remember, I am with you always, to the end of the age."*

The evangelization of the nations could only begin after the resurrection. After Jesus had taken away the sin and punishment of Israel and of the whole world, the good news of salvation could then go out to all peoples. The cross and resurrection, standing at the center of the world's history, give the course of humanity its meaning and direction. In this pivotal event, the human situation is radically renewed. In the resurrection, Jesus becomes, as Paul writes, the "firstborn" from the dead, the "firstfruits" of the new creation. The risen Lord is the first experience of something that will one day fill the whole world, and through him the powers of the age to come flow into the present.

So Jesus, risen and eternally alive, gives his disciples the great commission. Each of the four gospels concludes with the risen Jesus commissioning the community of his disciples to bring the good news to all nations (Matt 28:16–20; Mark 16:15–18; Luke 24:45–49; John 20:21–23). Yet Jesus does not present this evangelizing mission simply as a command to be obeyed. Rather, it is the result of knowing the good news and is produced by God's own Spirit. This mission to all peoples is the identity of the community Jesus founded. Evangelization is the overflow of the great gift of salvation.

The grand finale of Matthew's gospel occurs in Galilee on a mountain. The eleven disciples respond with reverence when they see Jesus, and they worship him (verse 17). Yet some of them also doubt, a word that connotes uncertainty and hesitation at this first encounter with the Risen One. This mixture of adoration and doubt, of faith and indecision, is characteristic of Christian discipleship until the close of the age.

The risen Jesus proclaims the universality of the authority bestowed upon him by the Father: "all authority in heaven and on earth" (verse 18). The declaration echoes the text of Daniel 7:14, concerning the exalted Son of Man: "To him was given dominion and glory and kingship, that all peoples, nations, and languages should serve him. His dominion is an everlasting dominion that shall not pass away, and his kingship is one that shall never be destroyed." The glory of Jesus as the risen and exalted Lord indicates that the final age is upon the earth, the anticipation of his final coming in glory.

The universal lordship of Jesus means a universal mission for his church. In Daniel 7 and in the climax of Matthew's gospel, the authority of the Son of Man is given over to his community (Dan 7:18, 22, 27). Because the authority of Jesus has been made universal by his resurrection, Jesus directs his church to a worldwide mission (verse 19). He commissions them to "go" to the nations. The people of the world will not come unless the disciples go to them.

The central responsibility of the disciples is to reproduce themselves, to make disciples. The commissioning reflects the threefold mission of the church: evangelization, baptism, and teaching. The initial task is the proclamation of the good news. Then new disciples are brought into the life of the church through baptism. Finally, detailed teaching in the way of Christ must form and guide new disciples.

This entire mission of the church is possible only because of the promise of the risen Lord: "I am with you always, to the end of the age" (verse 20). Though the responsibilities of disciples are daunting, the resources that are available to them in Jesus' authority and presence are more than adequate for the task. The disciples will experience his abiding presence in his church through the same Spirit that empowered Jesus during his public life. The presence of Jesus will give confidence to disciples in every age, guiding and confirming their decisions, as they await his coming again. Then he will reign over all humanity and all creation as the glorious king.

Reflection and discussion

- What is the threefold task that Jesus gave to his disciples? In what ways does the church continue this mission today?

- Why is the promise of Jesus, "I am with you always, to the end of the age," so foundational for missionary discipleship today?

Prayer

Risen Lord, who is given dominion and glory and kingship, I believe that all peoples, nations, and languages should serve your kingdom. Make me your missionary disciple, and help me to trust that your dominion is everlasting and will never pass away.

"The Spirit of the Lord is upon me, because he has anointed me to bring good news to the poor. He has sent me to proclaim release to the captives and recovery of sight to the blind, to let the oppressed go free." LUKE 4:18

The Mission of Jesus

LUKE 4:14–30 ¹⁴*Then Jesus, filled with the power of the Spirit, returned to Galilee, and a report about him spread through all the surrounding country.* ¹⁵*He began to teach in their synagogues and was praised by everyone.*

¹⁶*When he came to Nazareth, where he had been brought up, he went to the synagogue on the sabbath day, as was his custom. He stood up to read,* ¹⁷*and the scroll of the prophet Isaiah was given to him. He unrolled the scroll and found the place where it was written:*

¹⁸*"The Spirit of the Lord is upon me,*
because he has anointed me
to bring good news to the poor.
He has sent me to proclaim release to the captives
and recovery of sight to the blind,
to let the oppressed go free,
¹⁹*to proclaim the year of the Lord's favor."*

²⁰*And he rolled up the scroll, gave it back to the attendant, and sat down. The eyes of all in the synagogue were fixed on him.* ²¹*Then he began to say to them, "Today this scripture has been fulfilled in your hearing."* ²²*All spoke well of him and were amazed at the gracious words that came from his mouth. They said, "Is not this Joseph's son?"* ²³*He said to them, "Doubtless you will quote to me this proverb, 'Doctor, cure yourself!' And you will say, 'Do here also in your hometown*

the things that we have heard you did at Capernaum.'" ²⁴*And he said, "Truly I tell you, no prophet is accepted in the prophet's hometown.* ²⁵*But the truth is, there were many widows in Israel in the time of Elijah, when the heaven was shut up three years and six months, and there was a severe famine over all the land;* ²⁶*yet Elijah was sent to none of them except to a widow at Zarephath in Sidon.* ²⁷*There were also many lepers in Israel in the time of the prophet Elisha, and none of them was cleansed except Naaman the Syrian."* ²⁸*When they heard this, all in the synagogue were filled with rage.* ²⁹*They got up, drove him out of the town, and led him to the brow of the hill on which their town was built, so that they might hurl him off the cliff.* ³⁰*But he passed through the midst of them and went on his way.*

G uided and empowered by the Holy Spirit, Jesus went to Galilee where he began his public ministry by teaching in the synagogues of the area. The synagogues, as places where the Jewish people assembled for prayer, Scripture reading, instruction, and discussion, were the natural settings for Jesus to present his teachings. Since such instruction entailed primarily the interpretation of Scripture, and since Jesus was well versed in the Torah and prophets of Israel, he instructed the assembly at these Sabbath gatherings. His fame spread throughout the region, and he was praised by those who heard him.

As Jesus comes to his hometown of Nazareth, we see an example of the kind of teaching Jesus is offering throughout the synagogues of the region. He understands his own ministry as a natural completion of Judaism's hope, so he desires all Jews to enter this time of fulfillment. In the passage that he reads from the scroll of the prophet Isaiah, the Servant of the Lord announces release to all those in bondage (Isa 61:1–2). The liberation announced by the Servant is marked by four infinitives: to bring good news to the poor, to proclaim liberty to captives and sight to the blind, to let the oppressed go free, and to proclaim the year of the Lord's favor.

At the time of Jesus, the Jewish people would have understood this passage to refer to the coming of God's new age of salvation, so its proclamation by Jesus catches the attention of his listeners as they wait to hear his instruction. As Jesus sat down, the customary position for teaching, he begins with the words, "Today this scripture has been fulfilled in your hearing" (verse 21).

He is stating that the total deliverance that Isaiah describes is now put into motion with his coming. Jesus himself is the truest Servant of the Lord. He is the one anointed with God's Spirit to be the bearer of God's salvation to his people.

Those who are poor, captive, blind, or oppressed understand their own needs and respond more directly and honestly to God's message of hope than those who are not so subjugated. The imagery of deliverance echoes the description of the Jubilee year (Lev 25:8–17), when debts were canceled and slaves were liberated. Jesus' announcement of "the year of the Lord's favor" indicates the arrival of the time when the spiritual debt of sin will be forgiven and when those held in the bondage of sickness and evil will be freed. The words and deeds of Jesus throughout the rest of Luke's gospel indicate that this proclamation of Isaiah is a prologue to his saving ministry.

After Jesus proclaimed the Scripture passage fulfilled, "all spoke well of him and were amazed" (verse 22). But then the mood of the crowd shifts dramatically. When the people of Nazareth demand that Jesus do the things in his hometown that he has done elsewhere, they become skeptical and then furious. Jesus recalls how the prophets of Israel were rejected by their own people. He offers examples from the lives of Elijah and Elisha, showing how the rejection of the prophets in Israel led them to go beyond the borders of their own people and into Gentile lands. Jesus is prophesying how those closest to him will refuse God's salvation, while others who are far away will receive it. By this point, "all in the synagogue were filled with rage" and wanted to hurl him off a cliff. God's blessing for the Gentiles was too much for his audience to bear, so they rejected his message and his ministry.

Reflection and discussion

- What seems to be the essence of Jesus' mission according to this scene?

- What seems to be the reason for the radical change of mood from the crowd in Nazareth? Have I experienced a similar response from those who are close to me?

- How does Jesus' instruction indicate that healing, forgiveness, and liberation are all aspects of God's salvation? How have I experienced these from Jesus?

- Since this passage serves as an outline for the mission of Jesus in the gospel, how is it also a pattern for missionary discipleship today?

Prayer

Servant of the Lord, who announces good news to the poor, captive, blind, and oppressed, I thank you for the salvation you offer to every person. Don't let me ever be jealous of your generosity to others, but help me accept with gratitude the grace you give to me.

**"Blessed are the eyes that see what you see!
For I tell you that many prophets and kings desired
to see what you see, but did not see it, and to
hear what you hear, but did not hear it."** LUKE 10:23–24

The Mission of Jesus' Disciples

LUKE 10:1–24 ¹*After this the Lord appointed seventy others and sent them on ahead of him in pairs to every town and place where he himself intended to go.* ²*He said to them, "The harvest is plentiful, but the laborers are few; therefore ask the Lord of the harvest to send out laborers into his harvest.* ³*Go on your way. See, I am sending you out like lambs into the midst of wolves.* ⁴*Carry no purse, no bag, no sandals; and greet no one on the road.* ⁵*Whatever house you enter, first say, 'Peace to this house!'* ⁶*And if anyone is there who shares in peace, your peace will rest on that person; but if not, it will return to you.* ⁷*Remain in the same house, eating and drinking whatever they provide, for the laborer deserves to be paid. Do not move about from house to house.* ⁸*Whenever you enter a town and its people welcome you, eat what is set before you;* ⁹*cure the sick who are there, and say to them, 'The kingdom of God has come near to you.'* ¹⁰*But whenever you enter a town and they do not welcome you, go out into its streets and say,* ¹¹*'Even the dust of your town that clings to our feet, we wipe off in protest against you. Yet know this: the kingdom of God has come near.'* ¹²*I tell you, on that day it will be more tolerable for Sodom than for that town.*

¹³*"Woe to you, Chorazin! Woe to you, Bethsaida! For if the deeds of power done in you had been done in Tyre and Sidon, they would have repented long ago, sitting*

51

in sackcloth and ashes. [14]But at the judgment it will be more tolerable for Tyre and Sidon than for you. [15]And you, Capernaum,

will you be exalted to heaven?

No, you will be brought down to Hades.

[16]"Whoever listens to you listens to me, and whoever rejects you rejects me, and whoever rejects me rejects the one who sent me."

[17]The seventy returned with joy, saying, "Lord, in your name even the demons submit to us!" [18]He said to them, "I watched Satan fall from heaven like a flash of lightning. [19]See, I have given you authority to tread on snakes and scorpions, and over all the power of the enemy; and nothing will hurt you. [20]Nevertheless, do not rejoice at this, that the spirits submit to you, but rejoice that your names are written in heaven."

[21]At that same hour Jesus rejoiced in the Holy Spirit and said, "I thank you, Father, Lord of heaven and earth, because you have hidden these things from the wise and the intelligent and have revealed them to infants; yes, Father, for such was your gracious will. [22]All things have been handed over to me by my Father; and no one knows who the Son is except the Father, or who the Father is except the Son and anyone to whom the Son chooses to reveal him."

[23]Then turning to the disciples, Jesus said to them privately, "Blessed are the eyes that see what you see! [24]For I tell you that many prophets and kings desired to see what you see, but did not see it, and to hear what you hear, but did not hear it."

Jesus appoints seventy of his disciples and sends them out on a mission. They go ahead of him, two-by-two for mutual support, to prepare the regions where he intends to go. Like the number twelve, representing the twelve tribes of Israel, the number seventy is also related to the origins of Israel. During the journey of exodus, God told Moses to gather seventy of the elders of Israel (Num 11:16–17). These seventy received some of the spirit God had given to Moses, and they assisted Moses in leading the people. These seventy disciples of Jesus represent him when he is absent, and they carry out what will be the work of the church.

Although the disciples sometimes experience rejection, they also receive much positive response to the good news they proclaim. The plentiful harvest is the image used by Jesus for their successful missionary work. Yet because there are not enough laborers to reap the harvest, Jesus tells his disciples to ask God, "the Lord of the harvest," to call forth more men and women to serve with them so that the missionary task will grow. As people receive the gospel, they will take responsibility for it and help deliver it to others.

The mission Jesus gives to his missionary disciples is filled with risk. They go as vulnerable lambs into the midst of wolves but always by his authority and as his representatives. They must travel light and single-mindedly press on to their goal, without a hint of pretension, while relying on God's help and protection. Jesus explains that when they enter a house, they must extend a blessing of peace, offering God's grace, mercy, and salvation (verse 5). If the blessing is received with an open heart, it extends God's peace to the receiver. If it is rejected, it returns to the sender so that it can be given to someone more receptive (verse 6). The blessings brought by the laborers for God's kingdom are worthy of a wage of food and shelter from those who receive them (verse 7). And finally, Jesus tells these disciples how to respond to acceptance and how to respond to rejection.

The message of these disciples to those who receive them is this: "The kingdom of God has come near to you" (verse 9). With the coming of Jesus, God extends his saving power upon people in the face of all opposing forces. God's kingdom is inaugurated in the coming of the Messiah, and God's future reign is guaranteed. Since nothing can stop God's kingdom from coming, and the signs of the kingdom are already here, it is time for all people to receive it and enter into God's reign.

People can refuse God's offer of salvation, but such refusal is the worst form of negligence. Those who reject God's offer of deliverance from the effects of sin and death will experience inevitable judgment. Jesus expresses prophetic woes upon the cities where people have failed to respond to the gospel proclaimed by Jesus and his disciples (verse 13). Warning of the nearness of judgment and calling them to repentance, Jesus exclaims his anguish and pity for those who refuse the salvation he offers. In fact, Sodom, Tyre, and Sidon, notoriously wicked cities condemned by the ancient prophets, are better off than Chorazin, Bethsaida, and Capernaum, whose people refused God's offer of grace and failed to respond to the gospel of God's kingdom. The stinging rebuke emphasizes how sin can blind people in the face of God's mercy and forgiveness.

When the seventy disciples return to Jesus, they are rejoicing over the success of their mission (verse 17). They address Jesus as Lord and acknowledge that they have ministered in his name. Even demons are subject to them because they represent Jesus and share in his power. In a prophetic vision, Jesus sees Satan fall from heaven like a flash of lightning. Clearly, the disciples' ministry spells defeat for Satan. In fact, the disciples can overcome anything that opposes them through the authority of Jesus. The power of the evil one cannot remove their secure position before God or erase their names from God's book of life.

Jesus expresses deep joy and wonder at the results of his disciples' mission (verse 21). His spontaneous prayer expresses his gratitude to the Father for revealing the ways of the kingdom to those who are simple and open-hearted, unimpeded by preconceived ideas of how God should act. God's "gracious will" has always worked in this way: resisting the proud and giving grace to the humble. Although God freely gives, the attitude of the receiver determines the internal effects of that grace. The Father has entrusted everything to his Son, so Jesus is the channel of God's revelation and can make him known to anyone (verse 22). No one can truly understand the Father's saving will without listening to his Son. The prophets and kings of ancient Israel longed to see and hear the wonders of this age of salvation brought by Jesus (verses 23–24). How honored and blessed are all disciples who live in the time of fulfillment!

Reflection and discussion

- What is the purpose of traveling light and traveling in pairs for missionary disciples?

- Why does Jesus use the image of the plentiful harvest and the need for laborers to describe the mission he gives to his disciples?

- What indicates that people are ripe for the harvest? How am I being sent out as a laborer into the harvest?

- Why do some accept and others reject the blessing of peace, mercy, and salvation offered by the disciples of Jesus?

Prayer

I thank you, Father, Lord of heaven and earth, that I am blessed to experience what ancient prophets and kings only longed for. Thank you for revealing your kingdom to me and for the privilege of living in the age of Christ's church.

"Thus it is written, that the Messiah is to suffer and to rise from the dead on the third day, and that repentance and forgiveness of sins is to be proclaimed in his name to all nations, beginning from Jerusalem."

LUKE 24:46–47

Proclaim the Gospel to All Nations

LUKE 24:44–53 ⁴⁴*Then he said to them, "These are my words that I spoke to you while I was still with you—that everything written about me in the law of Moses, the prophets, and the psalms must be fulfilled." ⁴⁵Then he opened their minds to understand the scriptures, ⁴⁶and he said to them, "Thus it is written, that the Messiah is to suffer and to rise from the dead on the third day, ⁴⁷and that repentance and forgiveness of sins is to be proclaimed in his name to all nations, beginning from Jerusalem. ⁴⁸You are witnesses of these things. ⁴⁹And see, I am sending upon you what my Father promised; so stay here in the city until you have been clothed with power from on high."*

⁵⁰*Then he led them out as far as Bethany, and, lifting up his hands, he blessed them. ⁵¹While he was blessing them, he withdrew from them and was carried up into heaven. ⁵²And they worshiped him, and returned to Jerusalem with great joy; ⁵³and they were continually in the temple blessing God.*

At the conclusion of Luke's gospel, the risen Savior reaffirms the necessity of his suffering and resurrection in God's plan. His mission is the heart of the ancient Scriptures, although it is not explicitly described in the Old Testament. He is the fulfillment of everything written about him "in the law of Moses, the prophets, and the psalms" (verse 44). Jesus opens the disciples' minds by opening the Scriptures to them. In light of the resurrection, the minds of the disciples are opened to a new and deeper understanding of the ancient texts. They are now able to understand how the Old Testament teachings fit together and are completed in the dying and rising of Jesus the Messiah.

Jesus summarizes God's fundamental plan as revealed in Scripture with three infinitives: to suffer, to rise, and to proclaim (verses 46–47). The Scriptures teach that the Messiah would suffer and rise from the dead, and that a message of repentance and forgiveness would be proclaimed to all nations as a result. The first two of these elements of God's plan have just been completed, and the last remains for the disciples to carry out.

Jesus then commissions his disciples for the decisive role they are to play in the new and final phase of salvation history: they are to be witnesses to Jesus Christ, proclaiming repentance and forgiveness, beginning in Jerusalem and extending to the whole world. It is this witness of the disciples that is the subject of Luke's second volume, the Acts of the Apostles. The goal of Jesus' journey to Jerusalem now becomes the starting point from which the message of salvation will extend to the ends of the earth (Acts 1:8).

Finally, before his ascension to the Father, Jesus promises to send the Holy Spirit upon his disciples. Although his resurrection appearances have come to an end, the church will continue to experience his glorified presence and activity in many ways. Luke's sequel volume will continue the story of the church, beginning with the descent of the Holy Spirit and the empowerment of the disciples as witnesses to all the nations. The energy of God's Spirit, emanating from the resurrection, will empower the church to evangelize the world.

Reflection and discussion

- Why is it so critically important to study "the law of Moses, the prophets, and the psalms" in order to understand the significance and mission of Jesus?

- In what sense is Luke's gospel incomplete? What is necessary to complete it?

- In what ways is the church a witness to Jesus Christ in the world today? How is my life a part of that witness?

Prayer

Risen Savior, open my mind to understand the Scriptures, and give me the insight to see your presence in the ancient texts of Israel. Send your Holy Spirit upon me so that I may be empowered to be your witness.

SUGGESTIONS FOR FACILITATORS, GROUP SESSION 3

1. Welcome group members and ask if there are any announcements anyone would like to make.

2. You may want to pray this prayer as a group:
   Creating and redeeming God, your divine plan for the world's salvation comes to its climax in the life, death, and resurrection of Jesus, your Son, but it is only completed through the missionary discipleship of your people. We are blessed to experience in Jesus what the ancient prophets and kings only longed for. Thank you for revealing your kingdom to us and for the privilege of living in the age of your Holy Spirit as evangelizers to the nations. As we gather to study your word in the Bible, inspire new hope within us, assure us of your presence, and guide us in your will.

3. Ask one or more of the following questions:
   - Which message of Scripture this week speaks most powerfully to you?
   - What is the most important lesson you learned through your study this week?

4. Discuss lessons 7 through 12. Choose one or more of the questions for reflection and discussion from each lesson to discuss as a group. You may want to ask group members which question was most challenging or helpful to them as you review each lesson.

5. Remember that there are no definitive answers for these discussion questions. The insights of group members will add to the understanding of all. None of these questions require an expert.

6. After talking about each lesson, instruct group members to complete lessons 13 through 18 on their own during the six days before the next group meeting. They should write out their own answers to the questions as preparation for next week's group discussion.

7. Ask the group if anyone is having any particular problems with the Bible study during the week. You may want to share advice and encouragement within the group.

8. Conclude by praying aloud together the prayer at the end of one of the lessons discussed. You may add to the prayer based on the sharing that has occurred in the group.

They said to him, "Rabbi…where are you staying?"
He said to them, "Come and see." They came and saw where
he was staying, and they remained with him that day.

JOHN 1:38–39

The Invitation to Discipleship

JOHN 1:35–51 ³⁵*The next day John again was standing with two of his disciples, ³⁶and as he watched Jesus walk by, he exclaimed, "Look, here is the Lamb of God!" ³⁷The two disciples heard him say this, and they followed Jesus. ³⁸When Jesus turned and saw them following, he said to them, "What are you looking for?" They said to him, "Rabbi" (which translated means Teacher), "where are you staying?" ³⁹He said to them, "Come and see." They came and saw where he was staying, and they remained with him that day. It was about four o'clock in the afternoon. ⁴⁰One of the two who heard John speak and followed him was Andrew, Simon Peter's brother. ⁴¹He first found his brother Simon and said to him, "We have found the Messiah" (which is translated Anointed). ⁴²He brought Simon to Jesus, who looked at him and said, "You are Simon son of John. You are to be called Cephas" (which is translated Peter).*

⁴³*The next day Jesus decided to go to Galilee. He found Philip and said to him, "Follow me." ⁴⁴Now Philip was from Bethsaida, the city of Andrew and Peter. ⁴⁵Philip found Nathanael and said to him, "We have found him about whom Moses in the law and also the prophets wrote, Jesus son of Joseph from Nazareth." ⁴⁶Nathanael said to him, "Can anything good come out of Nazareth?" Philip said to him, "Come and see." ⁴⁷When Jesus saw Nathanael coming toward him, he said*

of him, "Here is truly an Israelite in whom there is no deceit!" ⁴⁸Nathanael asked *him, "Where did you get to know me?" Jesus answered, "I saw you under the fig tree* *before Philip called you." ⁴⁹Nathanael replied, "Rabbi, you are the Son of God! You* *are the King of Israel!" ⁵⁰Jesus answered, "Do you believe because I told you that* *I saw you under the fig tree? You will see greater things than these." ⁵¹And he said* *to him, "Very truly, I tell you, you will see heaven opened and the angels of God* *ascending and descending upon the Son of Man."*

In John's gospel, disciples of Jesus are often brought to him through the efforts of another. As John the Baptist points his disciples to Jesus, he announces that Jesus is the Lamb of God (verse 36). This marks the end of John's role in salvation history, and two of his disciples begin to follow Jesus. John the Baptist is not only a crucial witness to Jesus, but also the source from which Jesus drew his first followers.

The invitation to discipleship, like nearly every incident in John's gospel, contains multiple levels of meaning. The apparently casual question asked by Jesus of those following him, "What are you looking for?" (verse 38), is also probing and challenging. Jesus is really asking them if they know what they are searching for, if they know the meaning and purpose of their lives. We must realize that Jesus is also asking us the same question, as we seek to enter a deeper relationship with Jesus through this gospel.

Likewise, the question of the disciples, "Where are you staying?" (verse 38), and the response of Jesus, "Come and see" (verse 39), are an inquiry about the residence of this new teacher and an invitation to his home. But at a more profound level, the disciples are asking Jesus about his true home, where his heart is rooted, and Jesus invites them to come and experience his life, to abide with him and learn from him so that they can discover the truth about God's love. The same invitation is ours, as we respond to the invitation to follow Jesus and experience his life through this gospel.

The first precondition of discipleship is a profound yearning for deeper life. Jesus sees in these disciples not only who they are now, but the persons they will become. Jesus looks at Simon and sees that he will become Cephas, the Rock (verse 42). He looks at Nathaniel and sees "an Israelite in whom there is no deceit" (verse 47). Andrew, Simon Peter, Philip, and Nathaniel are all invited to "come and see." They come to know that Jesus too is more than he appears. On the surface, Jesus is the "son of Joseph from Nazareth" (verse 45), but he is also the Lamb of God (verse 36), the Messiah (verse 41), the one about whom Moses and the prophets wrote (verse 45), the Son of God, and King of Israel (verse 49).

Jesus promises these early disciples that they have far more to experience and comprehend: "Very truly, I tell you, you will see heaven opened and the angels of God ascending and descending upon the Son of Man" (verse 51). Jesus is alluding to Jacob's dream of the ladder reaching to heaven, with the angels ascending and descending upon it (Gen 28:12), assuring Jacob of God's fidelity. Jesus is telling his disciples that he himself is the place where God is revealed, where heaven and earth are joined, where God and humankind meet. Jesus is the culmination of divine revelation, providing a fullness of God's self-disclosure about which Jacob (later named Israel) could only dream. This divine manifestation will be seen in the seven ensuing "signs" of John's gospel and finally at the cross, the revelation of God's glory in Jesus Christ.

Reflection and discussion

- What is the significance of the fact that nearly everyone who comes to Jesus does so on the basis of someone else's witness? Am I willing, like Andrew and Philip, to bring others to Jesus?

- What am I looking for? How can I accept the invitation of Jesus to "come and see"?

- What obstacles are preventing me from experiencing a fuller and deeper life of discipleship?

- In what sense are people today experiencing a profound yearning for deeper life? Why is this yearning the first precondition of discipleship?

Prayer

King of Israel, although people longed for your coming for centuries, you invite each person by name to come and experience your life. Thank you for linking heaven and earth and leading me to a deeper relationship with God and a fuller life in you.

"It is no longer because of what you said that we believe, for we have heard for ourselves, and we know that this is truly the Savior of the world." JOHN 4:42

The Samaritan Woman Carries the Good News

JOHN 4:27–42 ²⁷*Just then his disciples came. They were astonished that he was speaking with a woman, but no one said, "What do you want?" or, "Why are you speaking with her?" ²⁸Then the woman left her water jar and went back to the city. She said to the people, ²⁹"Come and see a man who told me everything I have ever done! He cannot be the Messiah, can he?" ³⁰They left the city and were on their way to him.*

³¹Meanwhile the disciples were urging him, "Rabbi, eat something." ³²But he said to them, "I have food to eat that you do not know about." ³³So the disciples said to one another, "Surely no one has brought him something to eat?" ³⁴Jesus said to them, "My food is to do the will of him who sent me and to complete his work. ³⁵Do you not say, 'Four months more, then comes the harvest'? But I tell you, look around you, and see how the fields are ripe for harvesting. ³⁶The reaper is already receiving wages and is gathering fruit for eternal life, so that sower and reaper may rejoice together. ³⁷For here the saying holds true, 'One sows and another reaps.' ³⁸I sent you to reap that for which you did not labor. Others have labored, and you have entered into their labor."

³⁹Many Samaritans from that city believed in him because of the woman's testimony, "He told me everything I have ever done." ⁴⁰So when the Samaritans came to him, they asked him to stay with them; and he stayed there two days. ⁴¹And many more believed because of his word. [42] *They said to the woman, "It is no longer because of what you said that we believe, for we have heard for ourselves, and we know that this is truly the Savior of the world."*

After the encounter between the Samaritan woman and Jesus at the well of Samaria, the disciples return to Jesus and the Samaritan woman returns to her village. As the woman departs from the well to tell the good news, she leaves her water jar behind, an intriguing detail noted by the gospel writer (verse 28). Perhaps it conveys her haste to witness to Jesus, or perhaps it is the feminine counterpart to the male disciples leaving behind their nets and boats to follow Jesus. But the contrast between the male disciples and the woman could not be greater. While the men are "astonished that he was speaking with a woman" (verse 27), this astonishing woman has gone forth to tell others the good news of Jesus (verses 28–29). While the men are occupied with eating the food they have bought, the woman is evangelizing the Samaritans. While the disciples are trying to understand why Jesus doesn't seem hungry (verses 31–33), the Samaritans were already leaving their city to come to Jesus as a result of the woman's testimony (verse 30). Clearly this woman does the work of an evangelizer: proclaiming the good news, witnessing to Jesus, and bringing others to him.

The Samaritan woman's style of evangelizing can be a refreshing model for our own. She has no certain answers, no prepackaged formulas she tries to impose on her listeners. Her witness is invitational. She encourages others to "come and see" what she herself has experienced in Jesus (verse 29). Her faith is still tentative and undeveloped. She is still full of questions: "He cannot be the Messiah, can he?" She invites others to share in her searching. Though her belief is still hesitant and immature, she demonstrates an apostolic zeal, since it is impossible to keep such good news to oneself.

As the disciples are urging Jesus to eat something, Jesus states that he is sustained and nourished by doing the work of the Father: "My food is to do the will of him who sent me and to complete his work" (verse 34). Likewise, the "daily bread" of us who follow Jesus must be seeking God's will and carrying out the work he has given us. Even though we might maintain a balanced diet of physical food, we become malnourished unless we are sustained by a meaningful life in relationship to God. Jesus invites his disciples to the nourishing work of reaping the harvest that will result from what Jesus is sowing. Jesus tells them to look around and see the Samaritans coming to faith in him, like fields ripe for harvesting (verse 35). Jesus, sent by the Father (verse 34), in turn sends his disciples to continue his work (verse 38).

The Samaritan woman becomes the first evangelizer in John's gospel. Because she witnesses to others what she has experienced, other villagers come to meet Jesus and believe in him (verse 39). Then, as the Samaritans welcomed Jesus into their lives and spent time with him, "many more believed because of his word" (verse 41). They came to know and trust for themselves that Jesus is "truly the Savior of the world" (verse 42). Though the Samaritans must have seemed to the Jews of the time unlikely prospects for salvation, the seeds of grace are sown in unlikely places and reap fruit for eternal life (verse 36).

Reflection and discussion

- The Samaritan woman is the most effective evangelizer in the whole gospel. What does she have to teach disciples about witness and missionary endeavors?

- What does the woman's leaving behind her water jar indicate about Jesus' impact on her? What kind of an impact does she have on others?

- In what way is the witness of the Samaritan woman invitational? What makes her invitation so attractive to others?

- What new insights about missionary discipleship have emerged from my engagement with the story of the Samaritan woman?

Prayer

Savior of the world, you have sown the seed of your word within me through the labor of others before me. As my faith ripens for the harvest, you invite me to the mission of sowing your word in the hearts of others. May many others come to faith through the witness I offer.

"I have set you an example, that you also should do as I have done to you." JOHN 13:15

Love As I Have Loved You

JOHN 13:3–5, 12–17, 33–35 ³*Jesus, knowing that the Father had given all things into his hands, and that he had come from God and was going to God, ⁴got up from the table, took off his outer robe, and tied a towel around himself. ⁵Then he poured water into a basin and began to wash the disciples' feet and to wipe them with the towel that was tied around him.*

¹²*After he had washed their feet, had put on his robe, and had returned to the table, he said to them, "Do you know what I have done to you? ¹³You call me Teacher and Lord—and you are right, for that is what I am. ¹⁴So if I, your Lord and Teacher, have washed your feet, you also ought to wash one another's feet. ¹⁵For I have set you an example, that you also should do as I have done to you.¹⁶Very truly, I tell you, servants are not greater than their master, nor are messengers greater than the one who sent them. ¹⁷If you know these things, you are blessed if you do them.*

³³*"Little children, I am with you only a little longer. You will look for me; and as I said to the Jews so now I say to you, 'Where I am going, you cannot come.' ³⁴ I give you a new commandment, that you love one another. Just as I have loved you, you also should love one another. ³⁵By this everyone will know that you are my disciples, if you have love for one another."*

At his last meal with his disciples, Jesus performed an astonishing act: washing the feet of his disciples. This symbolic action summarizes the meaning of Jesus' whole life. On the night before his death, he shows them what his life has been about and what his death will mean. By washing the feet of his disciples, Jesus demonstrates that love is only real when it is expressed in loving service. John's gospel recounts Jesus' washing the feet of his disciples in place of the institution of the Eucharist, recounted during the Last Supper in the other gospels. Both actions express the self-giving of Jesus and his limitless love.

The unpaved roads got extremely dusty in dry weather and awfully muddy when it rained. Sandals gave little protection for the feet of travelers, so the servant of the house was always ready with a towel and washbowl to wash the feet of guests as they arrived. By taking the role of the servant, Jesus shocked his disciples with his humility and gave them a lesson they would not soon forget. In fact, this simple gesture has been memorialized by Christians through the ages as a prophetic demonstration of a disciple's lifestyle.

After washing his disciples' feet, Jesus explained his dramatic action: "If I, your Lord and Teacher, have washed your feet, you also ought to wash one another's feet" (verse 14). Jesus calls his symbolic action "an example," an act that his disciples must imitate for others (verse 15). The example of Jesus provides a model of self-giving and humble service. We are all called to love in this way. Such loving service will do more for humanity than all the power that we so often seek and honor.

But Jesus' action has another meaning, demonstrated by the objection of Peter and the disciples. Jesus is teaching them that discipleship means not only serving others but also learning how to be served by others. Accepting the loving care of others is also a mark of humble discipleship. Disciples have to learn to depend on others, to realize their need to be helped, before they are able to be true servants like Jesus.

The heart of Jesus' instructions to his followers is contained in his new commandment that Jesus gives to his followers: "Just as I have loved you, you also should love one another" (verse 34). The commandment is at once very old and totally new. It is based on God's ancient commandment: "You shall love your neighbor as yourself" (Lev 19:18). It is new because the standard of love is now the love with which Jesus has loved us. Though God has shown his love for us in many ways in the past, no one could dream that it would reach the point where the Son of God would die for us. Yet love is more than a commandment; it is a gift. We could never observe the commandment were it not for the fact that we have been created to share in God's life, which is love itself.

Reflection and discussion

- Which is easier for me: serving others or being served by others? Why are both important for discipleship?

- If the standard of love is now the love with which Jesus has loved us (verse 34), what are some of the characteristics of this love?

- Jesus said to his disciples, "You also should do as I have done to you." Whose feet have I washed lately? What act of service could I do today to express love for another?

Prayer

Suffering Servant, who loves us totally and absolutely, help me to love as you loved, to serve as you served, and to give myself as you gave yourself completely. Teach me to wash the feet of those I am called to love.

"The Advocate, the Holy Spirit, whom the Father
will send in my name, will teach you everything, and remind you
of all that I have said to you." JOHN 14:26

Greater Works Than These

JOHN 14:12–31 ¹²*"Very truly, I tell you, the one who believes in me will also do the works that I do and, in fact, will do greater works than these, because I am going to the Father.* ¹³*I will do whatever you ask in my name, so that the Father may be glorified in the Son.* ¹⁴*If in my name you ask me for anything, I will do it.*

¹⁵*"If you love me, you will keep my commandments.* ¹⁶*And I will ask the Father, and he will give you another Advocate, to be with you forever.* ¹⁷*This is the Spirit of truth, whom the world cannot receive, because it neither sees him nor knows him. You know him, because he abides with you, and he will be in you.*

¹⁸*"I will not leave you orphaned; I am coming to you.* ¹⁹*In a little while the world will no longer see me, but you will see me; because I live, you also will live.* ²⁰*On that day you will know that I am in my Father, and you in me, and I in you.* ²¹*They who have my commandments and keep them are those who love me; and those who love me will be loved by my Father, and I will love them and reveal myself to them."* ²²*Judas (not Iscariot) said to him, "Lord, how is it that you will reveal yourself to us, and not to the world?"* ²³*Jesus answered him, "Those who love me will keep my word, and my Father will love them, and we will come to them and make our home with them.* ²⁴*Whoever does not love me does not keep my words; and the word that you hear is not mine, but is from the Father who sent me.*

²⁵*"I have said these things to you while I am still with you.* ²⁶*But the Advocate, the Holy Spirit, whom the Father will send in my name, will teach you everything, and remind you of all that I have said to you.* ²⁷*Peace I leave with you; my peace I*

give to you. I do not give to you as the world gives. Do not let your hearts be trou-
bled, and do not let them be afraid. ²⁸You heard me say to you, 'I am going away,
and I am coming to you.' If you loved me, you would rejoice that I am going to the
Father, because the Father is greater than I. ²⁹And now I have told you this before
it occurs, so that when it does occur, you may believe. ³⁰I will no longer talk much
with you, for the ruler of this world is coming. He has no power over me; ³¹but I
do as the Father has commanded me, so that the world may know that I love the
Father. Rise, let us be on our way."

In his farewell discourse at supper with his disciples, Jesus anticipates the effects of his own departure and prepares his disciples for life in the age of the Spirit. Jesus assures them that they are not worse off because he is leaving them. In fact, those who believe in him will not only do the works he has done, but they will do "greater works" than these (verse 12). The works of disciples will be "greater," not necessarily in value, but certainly in scope. The disciples will do the works of God on a much wider scale because they will bring the gospel to the whole world. Closely associated with this promise is Jesus' assurance that he will answer his disciples' prayers (verses 13–14). Because he is going to the Father, Jesus tells them, the glory of God, once seen in his own deeds, will be seen in the deeds of his church.

Jesus came into the world to reveal the ultimate truth, the truth of the Father's love experienced by Jesus and manifested in his life, death, and resurrection. We are invited to participate in this truth by becoming one with Jesus through faith. This is accomplished through the work of the Holy Spirit, whom Jesus calls the "Advocate" (verse 16) and "the Spirit of truth" (verse 17). The word translated as "Advocate" means literally "one called to the side of another." The role of the Holy Spirit is to assist the believer in discovering all the real and practical implications of the profound truth revealed by Jesus.

Jesus promises that he will come to them and remain with them through the presence of the Holy Spirit, "whom the world cannot receive because it neither sees him nor knows him" in the usual and worldly sense of these terms (verse 17). This Spirit of truth is experienced interiorly as an abiding presence by those who follow the glorified Jesus. In this way, even though Jesus is departing, he will not leave his disciples as orphans (verse 18). Because they have been born from above and have become children of the Father, they will experience the loving intimacy of God's family even more closely: "You will know that I am in my Father, and you in me, and I in you" (verse 20). Jesus departs from the world only to be closer to his disciples than ever before.

Judas asks Jesus why the disciples and the world see things so differently (verse 22). Jesus explains that those who do not accept God's loving invitation cannot experience the Spirit of truth, the ongoing presence and revelation of God. The Spirit is, first of all, a gift from God, but a gift that must be accepted through one's loving, active response to God's word. Contrary to outward appearances, Jesus and the Father will make their home with the disciples (verse 23) in and through the Holy Spirit, who will be with them forever.

Although Jesus taught his followers many things throughout his public ministry, they were unable to understand much of what he said because the heart of his truth would be revealed in his death and resurrection. Jesus told his disciples that the role of the Holy Spirit is to "teach you everything and remind you of all that I have said to you" (verse 26). The Spirit of truth will continue the teaching of Jesus and deepen within his disciples the transforming reality of his dying and rising. The Spirit will enable believers to experience Jesus days, years, or centuries after his earthly life.

The effect of the Spirit's work within believers is a profound sense of peace, well-being, and confidence, the kind of peace that the world cannot give (verse 27). The *pax Romana* (Roman peace), secured by the emperor Augustus during the lifetime of Jesus, was obtained and maintained by military might. The peace given by Jesus, in contrast, was not obtained by inflicting violence or maintained with force. This peace does not go away even in the midst of life's most difficult struggles.

Though the disciples are focused on their own sense of loss due to Jesus' imminent departure, Jesus says, "If you loved me, you would rejoice that I am going to the Father" (verse 28). It is better for Jesus and also for his followers, who will be able to draw on the assistance of both the exalted Christ and the indwelling Holy Spirit. Jesus urges his disciples to place their trust in God and in himself, and also to do all they can to overcome their fears and their doubts with confidence and fidelity.

Reflection and discussion

- What are some of the changes Jesus emphasizes for the disciples after his own departure?

- In what ways have I experienced the Holy Spirit teaching me and reminding me as I study the Scriptures?

- Of all the promises Jesus gives his disciples in these verses, which one means the most to me?

Prayer

Son of the Father, who promises peace that the world cannot give, let me see and know the Spirit of Truth who lives in me always. Help me to trust that you will do whatever I ask in your name so that your Father may be glorified.

"You did not choose me but I chose you. And I appointed you to go and bear fruit, fruit that will last, so that the Father will give you whatever you ask him in my name." JOHN 15:16

Chosen to Bear Fruit

JOHN 15:8–21 ⁸*"My Father is glorified by this, that you bear much fruit and become my disciples. ⁹As the Father has loved me, so I have loved you; abide in my love. ¹⁰If you keep my commandments, you will abide in my love, just as I have kept my Father's commandments and abide in his love. ¹¹I have said these things to you so that my joy may be in you, and that your joy may be complete.*

¹²*"This is my commandment, that you love one another as I have loved you. ¹³No one has greater love than this, to lay down one's life for one's friends. ¹⁴You are my friends if you do what I command you. ¹⁵I do not call you servants any longer, because the servant does not know what the master is doing; but I have called you friends, because I have made known to you everything that I have heard from my Father. ¹⁶You did not choose me but I chose you. And I appointed you to go and bear fruit, fruit that will last, so that the Father will give you whatever you ask him in my name. ¹⁷I am giving you these commands so that you may love one another.*

¹⁸*"If the world hates you, be aware that it hated me before it hated you. ¹⁹If you belonged to the world, the world would love you as its own. Because you do not belong to the world, but I have chosen you out of the world—therefore the world hates you. ²⁰Remember the word that I said to you, 'Servants are not greater than their master.' If they persecuted me, they will persecute you; if they kept my word, they will keep yours also. ²¹But they will do all these things to you on account of my name, because they do not know him who sent me."*

In his farewell discourse, Jesus speaks about his ongoing relationship with his disciples after his departure. Because disciples are sustained by a continuing relationship with Jesus, they will bear much fruit (verse 8). This "fruit" borne by disciples includes all the manifestations of growth in Christ: love of others, humility, self-giving, faithfulness, and service to others. This is the fruit that will last (verse 16). This fruitfulness gives glory to the Father and provides the world with the clearest evidence of discipleship.

Love, we might say, is the divine energy that binds the Father with Jesus, and Jesus with his followers (verse 9). Jesus teaches his disciples that because the Father has loved him and Jesus has loved his disciples, their task is essentially this: "Abide in my love." As Jesus responded to the Father's love with obedient, sacrificial love for others, so disciples must respond to the love of Jesus with obedient, self-giving love for one another (verse 10). All that Jesus asks of his followers can be summarized in one great commandment: "Love one another as I have loved you" (verse 12).

This energy of divine love—the Father for Jesus, Jesus for his disciples, and disciples for one another—assures us that the obedience demanded of disciples is not grudging compliance. The commandments of Jesus are not to be obeyed out of a sense of obligation or fear; rather, they are motivated by love, and their purpose is joy. This is the reason, Jesus tells his disciples, that he has given them his teachings: "so that my joy may be in you, and that your joy may be complete" (verse 11). This complete joy is an experience of God's life, the kind of lasting joy that no sadness or hardship in life can take away.

Abiding in the love of Jesus is not just a warm feeling or sentimental emotion. Abiding is not static; it means doing something. Loving one another means loving as Jesus loves. It means self-giving for others, even laying down one's life for one's friends (verse 13). This is the example Jesus sets, symbolically in the foot washing and climactically in his death on the cross.

Although Jesus has previously spoken of his disciples as servants, he now chooses another term to express the type of relationship he desires with those who follow him. He calls his disciples "friends" (verse 15). A master generally tells his servants only what they need to know to do their job: "the servant does not know what his master is doing." However, friendship means sharing knowledge and personal insight: "I have called you friends, because I have made known to you everything I have heard from my Father."

Only Moses, the greatest figure of the Hebrew Scriptures, was privileged to speak to God as a "friend" (Exod 33:11), a relationship that seemed unattainable to the average Israelite. Yet Jesus calls his disciples "friends," and like a true friend, Jesus shares the best of himself with his disciples. The relationship of servant and master is based on obligation and earned privileges, while the relationship of friends is rooted in freedom and generosity. The Father's love that we experience in Jesus is not something that we have earned or even asked for. Jesus says, "You did not choose me but I chose you" (verse 16). This unearned, undeserved gift of friendship gives disciples the freedom and the motivation we need to bear "fruit that will last."

While missionary discipleship means friendship with Jesus and love for others, the negative side of discipleship is hatred from the world. During Jesus' earthly ministry, he himself bore the brunt of the world's persecution. But when he is removed from the world, the world's hatred will inevitably turn toward his disciples (verse 18). The type of relationship that Jesus has with his Father and that the disciples have with Jesus is not viewed favorably by those who trust only in power, control, and coercion. In fact, "the world" of these servants of power will hate the friends of Jesus who "do not belong to the world" (verse 19). The way of the world, which says that force and domination are the way to happiness, is directly opposed to the way of loving service done in freedom. Because Jesus has chosen them out of the world and closely identified them with himself, people's response toward the disciples will mirror their response toward Jesus (verse 20). The more his followers become like him, the more evident it will become that, though they are "in the world," they are not "of the world."

Reflection and discussion

- What fruit am I bearing because I am a disciple of Jesus? In what way does my fruitfulness give glory to God?

- What do I find comforting and challenging about the fact that Jesus calls me his "friend"?

- What does this farewell discourse of Jesus teach me about the motivations, spirit, purpose, and goals of missionary discipleship?

- What negative responses have I received because I am identified as a friend of Jesus? What does it mean to be "in the world" but not "of the world"?

Prayer

Living Lord, who calls me friend, give me confidence in my mission to transform the world with your truth. Guide me in your Spirit, and help me comprehend the gospel in all its richness. Make me a person of hope, and enable me to entrust my future to you.

"I ask not only on behalf of these, but also on behalf of those who will believe in me through their word, that they may all be one."

JOHN 17:20–21

I Have Sent Them into the World

JOHN 17:11–26 [11]*"Holy Father, protect them in your name that you have given me, so that they may be one, as we are one.* [12]*While I was with them, I protected them in your name that you have given me. I guarded them, and not one of them was lost except the one destined to be lost, so that the scripture might be fulfilled.* [13]*But now I am coming to you, and I speak these things in the world so that they may have my joy made complete in themselves.* [14]*I have given them your word, and the world has hated them because they do not belong to the world, just as I do not belong to the world.* [15]*I am not asking you to take them out of the world, but I ask you to protect them from the evil one.* [16]*They do not belong to the world, just as I do not belong to the world.* [17]*Sanctify them in the truth; your word is truth.* [18]*As you have sent me into the world, so I have sent them into the world.* [19]*And for their sakes I sanctify myself, so that they also may be sanctified in truth.*

[20]*"I ask not only on behalf of these, but also on behalf of those who will believe in me through their word,* [21]*that they may all be one. As you, Father, are in me and I am in you, may they also be in us, so that the world may believe that you have sent me.* [22]*The glory that you have given me I have given them, so that they may be one, as we are one,* [23]*I in them and you in me, that they may become completely one, so that the world may know that you have sent me and have loved them even as you have loved me.* [24]*Father, I desire that those also, whom you have given me, may be*

with me where I am, to see my glory, which you have given me because you loved me before the foundation of the world.

²⁵*"Righteous Father, the world does not know you, but I know you; and these know that you have sent me.* ²⁶*I made your name known to them, and I will make it known, so that the love with which you have loved me may be in them, and I in them."*

I n the final part of Jesus' last discourse, he turns from addressing his disciples to address his Father. And although Jesus lifts his eyes to heaven, he certainly wants his disciples (and all of us) to eavesdrop on this intimate conversation. In his parting prayer to the Father, he prays for his disciples. His own mission in the world is coming to an end, but that of the disciples is about to begin (verse 18). They have been "sent" into the world by Jesus, just as Jesus had been "sent" into the world by his Father.

As Jesus prays for his disciples, first he asks that God "protect them" from evil (verses 11, 15). As Jesus departs and leaves his disciples behind, he knows that they will be persecuted by the world, just as he himself was hated by the world (verse 14). Yet Jesus does not ask the Father to take them out of the world but rather to protect them from the evil powers within the world (verse 15). They no more belong to the world than he himself does, yet Jesus knows that they will still be physically present there even when he is not (verse 16). On the one hand, Jesus does not want them to withdraw from the world into an otherworldly enclave, but, on the other hand, he does not want them to become indistinguishable from the world.

Jesus then prays that God make them holy. To prepare them for success in their mission in the world, Jesus prays that God "sanctify," or make holy, his disciples "in the truth" (verses 17, 19). In his redeeming death, his self-gift of love on the cross, Jesus makes himself a holy sacrifice. He is both the priest offering the sacrifice for the sake of others and the sacrificial victim for others: "I sanctify myself, so that they also may be sanctified in truth."

As Jesus concludes his priestly prayer to the Father, his vision transcends the present. He prays not only for the disciples gathered around him, but also for all future believers who do not yet know him. This prayer includes all of us: those who will believe in Jesus through the word of his disciples (verse 20). He prays for the unity of all disciples throughout all of history, "that they may be one" (verse 21).

This oneness for which Jesus prays is not self-generated by the disciples. It is, rather, a deep unity established among believers by being taken into the oneness of love that Jesus has shared eternally with the Father (verse 22). This unity will be not only a satisfying harmony for believers, but it will be a powerful witness to the world. Its purpose, Jesus says, is to confirm his mission and the love of the Father: "So that the world may know that you have sent me and have loved them" (verse 23).

When the church of Jesus Christ is united, it is able to give credible testimony to the Father, who is united with the Son and the Spirit in revealing himself and in transmitting divine salvation to the world. United in the Father's love, the church can express the same love with which he has loved his Son, and it can proclaim the good news of this love to a hostile world. Jesus asks that we who have experienced his love for the Father may accept our responsibility to draw others into the unity of love that constitutes the heart of the Trinity.

Jesus concludes his prayer to the Father by declaring his desire that his disciples be with him to see his glory, the glory that the Father gave him because of his love for the Son "before the foundation of the world" (verse 24). The glory that Jesus desires his beloved disciples to experience is rooted in the Father's love for the Son; it preceded the world and it will outlast the world. Although the world does not yet know God, Jesus will continue to make the Father known in the world through the Spirit and, in turn, through the disciples (verses 25–26). This everlasting love of God, which unites the Father and the Son and joins Jesus with his disciples, creates the new community of Christ's church and draws others to believe.

Reflection and discussion

- Why does Jesus pray this final prayer aloud to his Father?

- In what ways is unity different from conformity and uniformity? For what kind of unity does Jesus pray?

- Why does Jesus pray for unity among those who believe in him? In what ways is the church's disunity an obstacle to belief?

- What can I do to bring greater unity to my home, my parish, and my community?

Prayer

Lord of Love, who calls your disciples to holiness and unity, make your church one, holy, catholic, and apostolic. Make me an instrument of that unity for which you prayed so that my life may always give glory to you.

SUGGESTIONS FOR FACILITATORS, GROUP SESSION 4

1. Welcome group members and ask if anyone has any questions, announcements, or requests.

2. You may want to pray this prayer as a group:
   Father of our Lord Jesus Christ, you have called us to encounter your Son, to experience his life, and to be his missionary disciples. Continue to deepen our relationship with him, sanctify us in the truth, and teach us to wash the feet of others. Give us confidence in our mission, guide us with your Spirit to comprehend the gospel in all its richness, share with us the joy that the world cannot give, and make us holy disciples so that the world may come to believe.

3. Ask one or more of the following questions:
   - What is the most difficult part of this study for you?
   - What insight stands out to you from the lessons this week?

4. Discuss lessons 13 through 18. Choose one or more of the questions for reflection and discussion from each lesson to discuss as a group. You may want to ask group members which question was most challenging or helpful to them as you review each lesson.

5. Keep the discussion moving, but allow time for the questions that provoke the most discussion. Encourage the group members to use "I" language in their responses.

6. After talking over each lesson, instruct group members to complete lessons 19 through 24 on their own during the six days before the next group meeting. They should write out their own answers to the questions as preparation for next week's session.

7. Ask the group what encouragement they need for the coming week. Ask the members to pray for the needs of one another during the week.

8. Conclude by praying aloud together the prayer at the end of one of the lessons discussed. You may choose to conclude the prayer by asking members to pray aloud any requests they may have.

"You will receive power when the Holy Spirit has come upon you; and you will be my witnesses in Jerusalem, in all Judea and Samaria, and to the ends of the earth." ACTS 1:8

Witnesses to the Ends of the Earth

ACTS 1:4–11 ⁴*While staying with them, [Jesus] ordered them not to leave Jerusalem, but to wait there for the promise of the Father. "This," he said, "is what you have heard from me; ⁵for John baptized with water, but you will be baptized with the Holy Spirit not many days from now."*

⁶So when they had come together, they asked him, "Lord, is this the time when you will restore the kingdom to Israel?" ⁷He replied, "It is not for you to know the times or periods that the Father has set by his own authority. ⁸But you will receive power when the Holy Spirit has come upon you; and you will be my witnesses in Jerusalem, in all Judea and Samaria, and to the ends of the earth." ⁹When he had said this, as they were watching, he was lifted up, and a cloud took him out of their sight. ¹⁰While he was going and they were gazing up toward heaven, suddenly two men in white robes stood by them. ¹¹They said, "Men of Galilee, why do you stand looking up toward heaven? This Jesus, who has been taken up from you into heaven, will come in the same way as you saw him go into heaven."

In his gospel, Luke demonstrated that all the activities of Jesus were directed by the Holy Spirit, through whom Jesus had been conceived and by whom he had been anointed at his baptism. In Acts, Luke shows that the church is empowered and directed by the same Holy Spirit, through whom the church is conceived and in whom the church is baptized and anointed.

When the disciples meet with the risen Jesus, they are filled with hope and yearning. They want Jesus to finish the work he has begun, to fulfill his promise to restore God's kingdom (verse 6). The reply of Jesus is twofold: first, he tells them that they cannot know "the times or periods that the Father has set," ending their speculation about the end of the age (verse 7); and second, he tells them that they will be his "witnesses" in the world (verse 8). The promised kingdom will be fully restored as a gift in God's own time, but in the meantime, they are not to wait idly, but they are to be witnesses filled with hope in the promises Jesus has left them.

In the programmatic verse of Acts, Jesus commissions his apostles to be witnesses, first "in Jerusalem," then "in Judea and Samaria," and finally "to the ends of the earth" (verse 8). This opening-out of the gospel message to a continually wider audience forms the structure of the book. The good news of forgiveness and the manifestation of God's Spirit is offered first to the Jews in Jerusalem, then to an increasingly large circle of peoples. Paul's arrival in Rome at the end of Acts indicates that the witness to Christ has truly become universal, extending to all the nations.

The ascension of Jesus means that the disciples' understanding of the world is now different. They recognize that the one who has taught, healed, and loved them has been raised to rule with the world's Creator. In this new reality, the future is still to be fully realized; it is open-ended to the movements of God's Spirit. The disciples are not to stand gazing up toward heaven, for the presence of Jesus will be with them in the spiritual outpouring they will soon receive. They should return to Jerusalem to await their empowerment by the Holy Spirit for their witness, because the same Spirit who empowered Jesus will be present in his church.

Jesus could have stayed on earth longer, or even forever, but he departed in order to leave his work in the hands of his missionary church. The entire book of Acts demonstrates, then, that the work of Jesus continues in the church through the power of the Holy Spirit. As Acts presents the church, it is made up of all kinds of people: Jews and Gentiles, the alienated and outcasts, apostles and martyrs. From Jerusalem to Rome, the people of God grow in number and devotion. The gospel reaches into the lives of every imaginable kind of person as disciples of Jesus learn that no one is excluded from God's desire to offer the gift of salvation to all.

In Luke's second volume, we see that Jesus is not a hero from the past; he is the Lord of the present. Though established in his heavenly abode, Jesus continues to be present to his church on earth, empowering his disciples to act on his behalf to continue the mission he began. The community of disciples is led by the Holy Spirit, living faithfully in a way that serves others, and sent to proclaim the gospel through the words and deeds of their lives.

Reflection and discussion

- How does the Holy Spirit provide the link between Luke's gospel and the Acts of the Apostles?

- Why do the men in white tell the disciples not to remain looking heavenward? What is the task of disciples between the time of Jesus' ascension and his return in glory?

- Do I seek Jesus by gazing to heaven or by doing his work on earth? What part of his mission has Jesus entrusted to me?

Prayer

Ascended Lord, send your Holy Spirit to me so that I may understand your word and proclaim it through my life. Empower me to be your witness and to continue your work in the world today.

Then Philip began to speak, and starting with this scripture, he proclaimed to him the good news about Jesus. ACTS 8:35

Philip Evangelizes the Ethiopian

ACTS 8:26–40 ²⁶*Then an angel of the Lord said to Philip, "Get up and go toward the south to the road that goes down from Jerusalem to Gaza." (This is a wilderness road.) ²⁷So he got up and went. Now there was an Ethiopian eunuch, a court official of the Candace, queen of the Ethiopians, in charge of her entire treasury. He had come to Jerusalem to worship ²⁸and was returning home; seated in his chariot, he was reading the prophet Isaiah. ²⁹Then the Spirit said to Philip, "Go over to this chariot and join it." ³⁰So Philip ran up to it and heard him reading the prophet Isaiah. He asked, "Do you understand what you are reading?" ³¹He replied, "How can I, unless someone guides me?" And he invited Philip to get in and sit beside him. ³²Now the passage of the scripture that he was reading was this:*

"Like a sheep he was led to the slaughter,
and like a lamb silent before its shearer,
so he does not open his mouth.
³³*In his humiliation justice was denied him.*
Who can describe his generation?
For his life is taken away from the earth."

³⁴*The eunuch asked Philip, "About whom, may I ask you, does the prophet say this, about himself or about someone else?" ³⁵Then Philip began to speak, and starting with this scripture, he proclaimed to him the good news about Jesus. ³⁶As they were going along the road, they came to some water; and the eunuch said, "Look, here is*

water! What is to prevent me from being baptized?" ³⁸*He commanded the chariot to stop, and both of them, Philip and the eunuch, went down into the water, and Philip baptized him.* ³⁹*When they came up out of the water, the Spirit of the Lord snatched Philip away; the eunuch saw him no more, and went on his way rejoicing.* ⁴⁰*But Philip found himself at Azotus, and as he was passing through the region, he proclaimed the good news to all the towns until he came to Caesarea.*

The second stage of the church's mission, the witness in Judea and Samaria (1:8), begins as the church is dispersed beyond Jerusalem due to its persecution there. In going beyond the Jews in Jerusalem, Philip reaches out to the margins. The church's understanding of the boundaries of God's people is changing rapidly. As a result of Philip's witness in word and deed, many come to believe in the good news of God's kingdom and are baptized.

On the road leading from Jerusalem toward Gaza, Philip encounters an Ethiopian eunuch, the treasurer to the queen of Ethiopia. He is returning from Jerusalem to his home, which is south of Egypt and deeper into Africa. Through this Ethiopian, the ministry of Philip brings the gospel not only into the regions of Judea but even to a new continent.

Traveling along the wilderness road in his chariot, the Ethiopian is reading aloud from a scroll of the prophet Isaiah. God's Spirit prompted Philip to approach the chariot and ask the man if he comprehends what he is reading. The Ethiopian admits that he needs a guide and invites Philip into the chariot to lead him in a discussion about the meaning of the Isaian text (verses 30–31).

The passage with which they begin is that of Isaiah 53, a description of the Servant of the Lord. In the Judaism of the time, the rabbis discussed how the subject of the passage could be the prophet himself, the people of Israel personified, or the coming Messiah. When the Ethiopian asks who the passage is speaking about, Philip makes clear to him how the passage ultimately refers to Jesus Christ. Philip explains how Jesus is the Servant who suffered unjustly, and how his death, which seems like a tragic loss, resulted in everything being gained. Then, using as well other passages of Scripture, he proclaims to him the good news of salvation.

The Ethiopian is a man of much power and authority, yet he is humble enough to know that he does not understand the word of God, and so he is receptive to the truth. Philip's proclamation of the good news leads the Ethiopian to faith, and when they arrive at a place of water, the believing Ethiopian requests to be baptized. Both Philip and the Ethiopian go down into the water, and Philip baptizes the new convert. When they come out of the water, Philip's work is complete, and God's Spirit takes hold of him and brings him to new missions along the coast.

The evangelizing mission of the church is reaching out beyond Jerusalem, to Samaria and Judea, and increasingly to the ends of the earth. Philip's mission is divinely led, prodded by the Holy Spirit. In obedience to God, Philip has been led along a desert road to encounter, of all people, an Ethiopian eunuch. Responsive to the Spirit, Philip and other missionary disciples like him find themselves in the oddest of situations with the most surprising sorts of people. The text presents the stages of evangelization in the early church: the preaching of the good news of Jesus, the interpretation of the Scriptures as preparation, the profession of faith on the part of the believer, and the solemn entry into the water of baptism.

Reflection and discussion

- Philip's ministry indicates how the Holy Spirit impels the church outward, breaking down previously held boundaries. How does the church follow this same impulse of the Spirit today?

- What kinds of people are beyond my boundary of comfort and familiarity? How might God be inviting me to get to know and serve someone outside my comfort zone?

- Am I like the Ethiopian, requesting guidance to help me understand the Scriptures? Am I like Philip, taking advantage of opportunities to explain the Scriptures to others?

- In what ways does this account of Philip inspire me toward a deeper experience of missionary discipleship?

Prayer

Risen Lord, you send disciples to continue your mission in ways they don't expect. Help me not to set limits on where you might ask me to go, what you might ask me to do, or how you might ask me to serve you.

Immediately he began to proclaim Jesus in the synagogues,
saying, "He is the Son of God." ACTS 9:20

Paul Chosen by God to Evangelize

ACTS 9:1–22 ¹*Meanwhile Saul, still breathing threats and murder against the disciples of the Lord, went to the high priest* ²*and asked him for letters to the synagogues at Damascus, so that if he found any who belonged to the Way, men or women, he might bring them bound to Jerusalem.* ³*Now as he was going along and approaching Damascus, suddenly a light from heaven flashed around him.* ⁴*He fell to the ground and heard a voice saying to him, "Saul, Saul, why do you persecute me?"* ⁵*He asked, "Who are you, Lord?" The reply came, "I am Jesus, whom you are persecuting.* ⁶*But get up and enter the city, and you will be told what you are to do."* ⁷*The men who were traveling with him stood speechless because they heard the voice but saw no one.* ⁸*Saul got up from the ground, and though his eyes were open, he could see nothing; so they led him by the hand and brought him into Damascus.* ⁹*For three days he was without sight, and neither ate nor drank.*

¹⁰*Now there was a disciple in Damascus named Ananias. The Lord said to him in a vision, "Ananias." He answered, "Here I am, Lord."* ¹¹*The Lord said to him, "Get up and go to the street called Straight, and at the house of Judas look for a man of Tarsus named Saul. At this moment he is praying,* ¹²*and he has seen in a vision a man named Ananias come in and lay his hands on him so that he might regain his sight."* ¹³*But Ananias answered, "Lord, I have heard from many about this man, how much evil he has done to your saints in Jerusalem;* ¹⁴*and here he has authority from the chief priests to bind all who invoke your name."* ¹⁵*But the Lord*

said to him, "Go, for he is an instrument whom I have chosen to bring my name
before Gentiles and kings and before the people of Israel; [16]*I myself will show him*
how much he must suffer for the sake of my name." [17]*So Ananias went and entered*
the house. He laid his hands on Saul and said, "Brother Saul, the Lord Jesus, who
appeared to you on your way here, has sent me so that you may regain your sight
and be filled with the Holy Spirit." [18]*And immediately something like scales fell*
from his eyes, and his sight was restored. Then he got up and was baptized, [19]*and*
after taking some food, he regained his strength.

For several days he was with the disciples in Damascus, [20]*and immediately he*
began to proclaim Jesus in the synagogues, saying, "He is the Son of God." [21]*All*
who heard him were amazed and said, "Is not this the man who made havoc in
Jerusalem among those who invoked this name? And has he not come here for the
purpose of bringing them bound before the chief priests?" [22]*Saul became increas-*
ingly more powerful and confounded the Jews who lived in Damascus by proving
that Jesus was the Messiah.

S aul, who is also known as Paul, experiences one of history's most
remarkable conversions as he is transformed by God's power from
persecutor of the church to the church's greatest evangelizer and missionary. The event is so important for Luke's narrative in Acts that he gives
us three versions: once here and twice in Paul's defense speeches (22:6–11;
26:12–18), each offering some new aspect of the event's significance.

Paul's divine encounter is described as a flashing light, a divine voice, a
double calling of his name—an experience so intense that he falls to the
ground. Although he does not immediately realize it, Saul is seeing the glory
of the risen Jesus, resplendent in the glory of the Father, blinding his eyes. The
divine voice is that of Jesus, asking Saul, "Why do you persecute me?" (verse
4). The question suggests the corporate solidarity of Jesus with his church.
Then Paul's question, "Who are you, Lord?" to which the Lord replies, "I am
Jesus, whom you are persecuting," makes explicit the reality that Christ has
a tangible presence in his church. When Saul was persecuting the church, he
was persecuting Jesus himself.

Luke describes the young church with a number of terms and images in
this passage: the church is "the disciples of the Lord" (verse 1), "the Way"

(verse 2), the living presence of Jesus in the world (verse 5), the saints (verse 13), and "all who invoke [the name of the Lord]" (verses 14; 2:21). Saul's failure to destroy this movement and his radical transformation into its greatest advocate is a sure sign that Jesus is truly the risen Lord and that the movement comes from God. In due course Paul will be told what his mission will entail. But for now, Paul will go to Damascus. Unable to see because of his divine encounter, he is led by the hand of his companions into the city (verse 8). Blind and helpless, Paul is brought into Damascus, to the house of Judas on the street called Straight. For three days, he sits in darkness and fasts from food and drink in repentance.

Meanwhile, a disciple named Ananias, perhaps the leader of the church in Damascus, is told in a vision to come to the house where Paul is staying. Ananias is reluctant, having heard of all the havoc Saul had created for the church in Jerusalem and knowing that he has come to Damascus to arrest believers. But God assures Ananias, "Go, for he is an instrument whom I have chosen to bring my name before Gentiles and kings and before the people of Israel" (verse 15). Ananias then goes to the house, lays his hands on Saul, and heals his blindness. Then Saul is baptized into Jesus Christ.

Saul the persecutor, who was headed to Damascus with the intention of bringing back believers in Jesus to Jerusalem as prisoners, is now Saul the missionary disciple, sent with a commission from Jesus Christ. Although Saul will never completely forget his past, it has been forgiven, and God now has a true vocation for him. He needs the faith of a believer named Ananias and the gift of the Spirit through baptism in order to know what to do and to have the strength to do it.

Reflection and discussion

- What might Paul have been thinking and feeling during his three days of blindness?

- Why would Jesus have chosen Saul, a zealous enemy of the church, as his greatest missionary disciple?

- Why was Paul brought from a state of zealous certainty about his mission to persecute the church to the condition of blind helplessness? How did this experience prepare him for missionary discipleship?

- The early Christians referred to their path as missionary disciples as a journey—"the Way" (verse 2). How have I experienced the path of my discipleship as a journey under the call and leading of Jesus?

Prayer

Risen Lord, who transformed the life of your apostle Paul, work deeply within me to form me into a missionary disciple. Change my certainty to humility, my confusion to understanding, my complacency to zeal, and my apathy to love for your church.

"I truly understand that God shows no partiality, but in every nation anyone who fears him and does what is right is acceptable to him."

ACTS 10:34–35

Peter's Missionary Journey to Cornelius

ACTS 10:25–48 *²⁵On Peter's arrival Cornelius met him, and falling at his feet, worshiped him. ²⁶But Peter made him get up, saying, "Stand up; I am only a mortal." ²⁷And as he talked with him, he went in and found that many had assembled; ²⁸and he said to them, "You yourselves know that it is unlawful for a Jew to associate with or to visit a Gentile; but God has shown me that I should not call anyone profane or unclean. ²⁹So when I was sent for, I came without objection. Now may I ask why you sent for me?"*

³⁰Cornelius replied, "Four days ago at this very hour, at three o'clock, I was praying in my house when suddenly a man in dazzling clothes stood before me. ³¹He said, 'Cornelius, your prayer has been heard and your alms have been remembered before God. ³²Send therefore to Joppa and ask for Simon, who is called Peter; he is staying in the home of Simon, a tanner, by the sea.' ³³Therefore I sent for you immediately, and you have been kind enough to come. So now all of us are here in the presence of God to listen to all that the Lord has commanded you to say."

³⁴Then Peter began to speak to them: "I truly understand that God shows no partiality, ³⁵but in every nation anyone who fears him and does what is right is acceptable to him. ³⁶You know the message he sent to the people of Israel, preaching peace by Jesus Christ—he is Lord of all. ³⁷That message spread throughout Judea, beginning in Galilee after the baptism that John announced: ³⁸how God anointed

Jesus of Nazareth with the Holy Spirit and with power; how he went about doing good and healing all who were oppressed by the devil, for God was with him. ³⁹*We are witnesses to all that he did both in Judea and in Jerusalem. They put him to death by hanging him on a tree;* ⁴⁰*but God raised him on the third day and allowed him to appear,* ⁴¹*not to all the people but to us who were chosen by God as witnesses, and who ate and drank with him after he rose from the dead.* ⁴²*He commanded us to preach to the people and to testify that he is the one ordained by God as judge of the living and the dead.* ⁴³*All the prophets testify about him that everyone who believes in him receives forgiveness of sins through his name."*

⁴⁴*While Peter was still speaking, the Holy Spirit fell upon all who heard the word.* ⁴⁵*The circumcised believers who had come with Peter were astounded that the gift of the Holy Spirit had been poured out even on the Gentiles,* ⁴⁶*for they heard them speaking in tongues and extolling God. Then Peter said,* ⁴⁷*"Can anyone withhold the water for baptizing these people who have received the Holy Spirit just as we have?"* ⁴⁸*So he ordered them to be baptized in the name of Jesus Christ. Then they invited him to stay for several days.*

The house of Cornelius is the setting for the most momentous event of the apostolic age. As Peter walks through the open door of Cornelius' house, he takes the first step in opening the church to the Gentiles. Cornelius has prepared for Peter's arrival by inviting his close friends and relatives to listen to Peter. At his arrival, Cornelius considers Peter a messenger of God and falls at his feet in homage. But Peter graciously instructs Cornelius to stand up because he faces a fellow human being (verse 26). Whatever Peter has to offer this Gentile officer, he knows it does not come from himself.

At the house of Cornelius, God is breaking down the barriers that for so long have been assumed to be God's will. Peter tells the assembly of the risk he is taking: "You yourselves know that it is unlawful for a Jew to associate with or to visit a Gentile" (verse 28). The Jews had erected firm barriers against Gentiles because of the need to maintain the purity of their beliefs and to prevent them from being infiltrated by pagan doctrines and practices. But Peter goes on to explain that God has revised his understanding: "God has shown me that I should not call anyone profane or unclean." Peter now realizes that the barriers between Jews and Gentiles no longer serve their original purpose, as God is bringing about a new age of salvation for all in Jesus Christ.

For the first and last time in Acts, Peter addresses a Gentile audience. He begins with a stunning proclamation: "I truly understand that God shows no partiality" (verse 34). God treats everyone on the same basis, and people from every nation have the same potential access to God. Peter highlights only two characteristics of the person who is acceptable to God: "anyone who fears him and does what is right" (verse 35). In other words, those who treat God with reverence and treat people with justice are ready for the saving revelation of God through Jesus Christ.

This monumental statement of God's non-partiality among those he calls to faith reverberates down through the history of the church. God sends the Holy Spirit upon all who accept the good news, and God forbids human partiality or prejudice from limiting his saving work. The proclamation of the good news of Jesus Christ is effective for those who are ready to receive it. It becomes a saving message for those who are open and realize their need for God. Cornelius had been seeking God for a long time. He has already begun to pray and to do good for those in need. God has been preparing his mind and heart for the message he is now receiving from Peter. Now, as he listens to the gospel proclaimed by Peter, Cornelius moves from an open seeker to a confirmed believer.

Summarizing the essentials of the Christian message, Peter emphasizes that Jesus is "Lord of all" (verse 36). The great commission given by Jesus to his disciples, to preach the message of salvation "to all nations, beginning from Jerusalem" (Luke 24:47), is starting to be realized as the saving news extends beyond Jerusalem and is destined for all the nations of the world.

As Peter is still speaking, proclaiming forgiveness of sins to everyone who believes, the Holy Spirit is given to Cornelius and the other Gentiles who are listening to Peter (verse 44). The Jewish believers who have come with Peter are amazed that "the gift of the Holy Spirit" has been poured out "even on the Gentiles" (verse 45). The coming of God's promised Spirit is the sign of the new era, and this event has rightly been called the Pentecost of the Gentile world (verse 47).

Peter understands the significance of the moment and he instructs that the Gentiles be baptized in the name of Jesus Christ (verse 48).

In the house of Cornelius, God demonstrates that Jews and Gentiles are equal in Christ; their need and God's answer to that need are the same. Peter receives hospitality and shares table fellowship for several days with these uncircumcised Christians. He is God's primary instrument of this epoch-making work, showing that the Gentiles too are chosen for salvation, baptism, and membership in Christ's church. The way has been prepared for the gospel to go out into the entire world.

Reflection and discussion

- How does the conversion of Cornelius and his household express the four marks of the church: one, holy, catholic, and apostolic?

- Why is the encounter of Peter with Cornelius a climactic moment in the development of the early church?

- What walls of prejudice and division prevent the gospel from being truly universal today?

Prayer

Lord of all, you taught your church to transcend nations, races, genders, and all divisions. You know the ways in which my mind and heart need conversion. Lead me to see other people as you see them, and to offer them the love that you have for them.

**"He is not far from each one of us.
For 'In him we live and move and have our being.'"**
ACTS 17:27–28

Paul Proclaims the God of All People

ACTS 17:16–32 ¹⁶*While Paul was waiting for them in Athens, he was deeply distressed to see that the city was full of idols.* ¹⁷*So he argued in the synagogue with the Jews and the devout persons, and also in the marketplace every day with those who happened to be there.* ¹⁸*Also some Epicurean and Stoic philosophers debated with him. Some said, "What does this babbler want to say?" Others said, "He seems to be a proclaimer of foreign divinities." (This was because he was telling the good news about Jesus and the resurrection.)* ¹⁹*So they took him and brought him to the Areopagus and asked him, "May we know what this new teaching is that you are presenting?* ²⁰*It sounds rather strange to us, so we would like to know what it means."* ²¹*Now all the Athenians and the foreigners living there would spend their time in nothing but telling or hearing something new.*

²²*Then Paul stood in front of the Areopagus and said, "Athenians, I see how extremely religious you are in every way.* ²³*For as I went through the city and looked carefully at the objects of your worship, I found among them an altar with the inscription, 'To an unknown god.' What therefore you worship as unknown, this I proclaim to you.* ²⁴*The God who made the world and everything in it, he who is Lord of heaven and earth, does not live in shrines made by human hands,* ²⁵*nor is he served by human hands, as though he needed anything, since he himself gives to all mortals life and breath and all things.* ²⁶*From one ancestor he made all*

*nations to inhabit the whole earth, and he allotted the times of their existence and the boundaries of the places where they would live, *[27]*so that they would search for God and perhaps grope for him and find him—though indeed he is not far from each one of us. *[28]*For 'In him we live and move and have our being'; as even some of your own poets have said,*

> *'For we too are his offspring.'*

[29]*Since we are God's offspring, we ought not to think that the deity is like gold, or silver, or stone, an image formed by the art and imagination of mortals. *[30]*While God has overlooked the times of human ignorance, now he commands all people everywhere to repent, *[31]*because he has fixed a day on which he will have the world judged in righteousness by a man whom he has appointed, and of this he has given assurance to all by raising him from the dead."*

[32]*When they heard of the resurrection of the dead, some scoffed; but others said, "We will hear you again about this."*

In the days of Paul, Athens was still considered the intellectual capital of the Greco-Roman world, even though the golden age of Athens had passed. The city represented the philosophy and culture of ancient Greece and was filled with fine examples of art and architecture. As Paul walks through the Acropolis, the agora, and the streets of the city, he sees the representations of many gods in the temples, in the niches of buildings, and on street corners.

As a monotheistic Jew, Paul sees these not as objects of art but as idolatry, and he is deeply distressed by them. In this cosmopolitan city, Paul would have encountered a wide diversity of people, from the Jews who met in the synagogue to the variety of people from many nations whom he encountered in the marketplace (verse 17). As he contends with audiences, his message is misunderstood. Some of the philosophers accuse him of being a "babbler," literally, one who picks up bits of news as a bird pecks at seeds. They also accuse him of being "a proclaimer of foreign divinities," perhaps because he speaks of Jesus and resurrection (verse 18), which sounds to his hearers like a pair of new gods (in Greek, *Iesous* and *Anastasis*).

The philosophers and people of Athens bring Paul to the Areopagus, where Athenians gather to hear matters of legal, political, and religious significance. Asked to explain his new teaching, Paul fashions his response in a well-constructed piece of classical rhetoric. He does not condemn Greek teachings in order to replace them with the gospel. Instead, he argued that all people are groping for the truth about God. This search for truth—expressed in shrines and statues, poetry and philosophy—is a proper foundation for the revelation of the one God of all. His notice of an altar "to an unknown god" becomes the springboard for proclaiming "the God who made the world and everything in it, he who is Lord of heaven and earth" (verses 23–24).

The scene presents the most complete example in Acts of how Paul addresses a purely Gentile audience. Rather than base his arguments on the Jewish Scriptures, he forms his discourses from the tenets of Greek philosophy. He offers a model of how Jerusalem can speak to Athens, how divine revelation contained in Scripture can dialogue with the human reason of philosophy. Paul uses Greek writers as legitimate conversation partners in approaching the truth of the gospel. Christian teaching would continue to build on Greek philosophy in future ages: Augustine on Plato and Thomas Aquinas on Aristotle.

Speculative thinking, however, can only move people to the edges of faith. Philosophy can help people understand that divine revelation is reasonable, but it is not enough for belief. Human reason can create the springboard; but faith ultimately requires a leap. The God of all people, about whom Paul speaks, is also the living and personal God revealed in the tradition and Scriptures of Israel. Before this God all people must repent, and in this one God all people must come to believe. The resurrection of Jesus from the dead is humanity's assurance that this God is indeed the Lord of heaven and earth.

Reflection and discussion

- What is the relationship between reason and faith? Why are both necessary?

- Paul knew that all people have a built-in desire to know and worship God. What are some of the signs Paul saw in Athens of this human search for God?

- Missionary discipleship involves dialogue with people who are searching for truth and transcendence. In what ways is Paul's speech a model or example of how disciples can dialogue with seekers in the world today?

- What is the difference between Greek philosophy and the message of the gospel? How can philosophy prepare people to receive the gospel?

Prayer

God of heaven and earth, you are the one God in whom "we live and move and have our being." Because you have instilled a natural longing for you in the hearts of all people, all people in some way search for you. Help me to trust that you are "not far from each of us."

From morning until evening he explained the matter to them,
testifying to the kingdom of God and trying to convince them
about Jesus both from the law of Moses and from the prophets.

ACTS 28:23

Paul Announces the Gospel in Rome

ACTS 28:16–31 ¹⁶*When we came into Rome, Paul was allowed to live by himself, with the soldier who was guarding him.*

¹⁷*Three days later he called together the local leaders of the Jews. When they had assembled, he said to them, "Brothers, though I had done nothing against our people or the customs of our ancestors, yet I was arrested in Jerusalem and handed over to the Romans.* ¹⁸*When they had examined me, the Romans wanted to release me, because there was no reason for the death penalty in my case.* ¹⁹*But when the Jews objected, I was compelled to appeal to the emperor—even though I had no charge to bring against my nation.* ²⁰*For this reason therefore I have asked to see you and speak with you, since it is for the sake of the hope of Israel that I am bound with this chain."* ²¹*They replied, "We have received no letters from Judea about you, and none of the brothers coming here has reported or spoken anything evil about you.* ²²*But we would like to hear from you what you think, for with regard to this sect we know that everywhere it is spoken against."*

²³*After they had set a day to meet with him, they came to him at his lodgings in great numbers. From morning until evening he explained the matter to them, testifying to the kingdom of God and trying to convince them about Jesus both from the law of Moses and from the prophets.* ²⁴*Some were convinced by what he*

had said, while others refused to believe. ²⁵*So they disagreed with each other; and as they were leaving, Paul made one further statement: "The Holy Spirit was right in saying to your ancestors through the prophet Isaiah,*

²⁶*'Go to this people and say,*
You will indeed listen, but never understand,
and you will indeed look, but never perceive.
²⁷*For this people's heart has grown dull,*
and their ears are hard of hearing,
and they have shut their eyes;
so that they might not look with their eyes,
and listen with their ears,
and understand with their heart and turn—
and I would heal them.'
²⁸*Let it be known to you then that this salvation of God has been sent to the Gentiles; they will listen."*

³⁰*He lived there two whole years at his own expense and welcomed all who came to him,* ³¹*proclaiming the kingdom of God and teaching about the Lord Jesus Christ with all boldness and without hindrance.*

After a series of arrests, trials, and escapes, Paul has arrived in Rome and is living under Roman guard. He has appealed his case in Jerusalem to the emperor in Rome; now he is awaiting trial. These final scenes of Acts describe Paul's proclamation of the gospel in Rome, but the book ends abruptly.

Within three days, Paul gathers the Jewish leaders of Rome, calling them "brothers" to emphasize his continuing unity with the Jewish community. Paul assures them that he has done nothing against his own people or their ancient traditions. He is wearing a Roman chain, not for any disloyalty to his people, but for his loyalty to the hope that they all share, "the hope of Israel" (verse 20).

After the Roman Jews express a desire to hear from Paul about the new Jewish sect that they have been hearing about, they meet with him in large numbers at his lodging (verse 23). He explains to them all day about Jesus the Messiah and the kingdom of God, basing his teachings on the Torah and prophets of Israel. The listeners disagree with one another; some believe and others refuse. And as they are departing, Paul reminds them of the warning that Isaiah had given to their ancestors. The eyes, ears, and hearts of God's people are closed and unresponsive to the new message of God (verses 26–27). They refuse to turn to God for their healing.

Acts ends on a note of triumph. Paul declares, "This salvation of God has been sent to the Gentiles; they will listen." Although Paul is in chains, the gospel cannot be chained. Though first directed to the Jews, the good news of salvation is now sent to everyone. Even though Paul is still a prisoner, he lives under house arrest in his own rented lodgings with a guard, welcoming everyone who comes to him. Confidently and unhindered, Paul continues to preach about the kingdom of God and to teach about the Lord Jesus Christ (verses 30–31). His door is always open to anyone who will listen to him and consider his message.

Luke's conclusion demonstrates that God has accomplished his plans: fulfilling the hope of Israel in Jesus and sharing that fulfillment with the world through Paul's witness "to the ends of the earth" (1:8). The gospel has been proclaimed from Jerusalem to Rome. Yet the conclusion is not the end of the story of Christ's church. The church is still preaching and teaching the word of God to whoever will open their eyes, ears, and heart to the salvation God is offering to all.

The abrupt ending leaves many details untold. It feels quite unfinished because the goal of the work, witnessing Jesus Christ to the ends of the earth, is incomplete. Luke wants readers to feel the incompleteness of the story and then take up the story in their own lives and continue working toward the goal. Although the second half of the book focuses on Paul, he remains just one instrument of God's work. The work is about the expansion of the good news of Jesus Christ and the growth of his church, led by the Holy Spirit. Paul's evangelizing ministry in Rome is the zenith of this development, the perfect conclusion of a narrative that repeatedly demonstrates the gospel crossing into new territory. But his work is certainly not the end of the church's witnessing to the ends of the earth. Acts is an unfinished book; it is still being written, we might say, by the ongoing work of missionary discipleship.

Where are the ends of the earth? From a first-century perspective, Rome is the center of the earth, not its end. For Jews, Greeks, and Romans, the world extended far beyond Rome: to Spain and Britain in the west, Scythia in the north, India in the east, and Ethiopia in the south. For the twenty-first-century disciple, the ends of the earth are wherever there are people who have not experienced God's saving love. For you and me, it is all around us. It is the responsibility of each believer to contribute to the evangelizing mission of the church. Luke's ending challenges you and me to press on with the unfinished task.

Reflection and discussion

- In what ways does Paul's example inspire me to be a missionary disciple of Jesus?

- How can closed eyes, ears, and hearts prevent people from experiencing God's salvation? Why do people close themselves from God's saving grace?

- In what ways does this unfinished book inspire and empower me to continue the mission?

Prayer

Lord Jesus, hope of Israel and light to the Gentiles, continue to pour out your Spirit so that I may continue the mission that you gave to your disciples. Stir up within me a passion for the gospel and a desire to evangelize the world around me through the witness of my life.

SUGGESTIONS FOR FACILITATORS, GROUP SESSION 5

1. Welcome group members and ask if anyone has any questions, announcements, or requests.

2. You may want to pray this prayer as a group:
   Messiah and Lord, who transformed the lives of your disciples through the coming of the Holy Spirit, work deeply within me to form me as a missionary disciple. Help me understand your word, empower me to be your witness, and free me to proclaim it through my life. Let me not set limits on where you might ask me to go, what you might ask me to do, or how you might ask me to serve you. Lead me to see other people as you see them, to offer them the love that you have for them, and to continue the mission that you gave to your disciples.

3. Ask one or more of the following questions:
   - What most intrigued you from this week's study?
   - Why is Luke's gospel often considered the good news of mercy and compassion?

4. Discuss lessons 19 through 24. Choose one or more of the questions for reflection and discussion from each lesson to talk over as a group.

5. Ask the group members to name one thing they have most appreciated about the way the group has worked during this Bible study. Ask group members to discuss any changes they might suggest in the way the group works in future studies.

6. Invite group members to complete lessons 25 through 30 on their own during the six days before the next meeting. They should write out their own answers to the questions as preparation for next week's session.

7. Discuss ways in which a better understanding of missionary discipleship could benefit the pastoral ministry within your community.

8. Conclude by praying aloud together the prayer at the end of one of the lessons discussed. You may want to conclude the prayer by asking members to voice prayers of thanksgiving.

"The one who formerly was persecuting us is now proclaiming the faith he once tried to destroy." GAL 1:23

Called to Proclaim Christ Among the Gentiles

GALATIANS 1:11–24 *¹¹For I want you to know, brothers and sisters, that the gospel that was proclaimed by me is not of human origin; ¹²for I did not receive it from a human source, nor was I taught it, but I received it through a revelation of Jesus Christ.*

¹³You have heard, no doubt, of my earlier life in Judaism. I was violently persecuting the church of God and was trying to destroy it. ¹⁴I advanced in Judaism beyond many among my people of the same age, for I was far more zealous for the traditions of my ancestors. ¹⁵But when God, who had set me apart before I was born and called me through his grace, was pleased ¹⁶to reveal his Son to me, so that I might proclaim him among the Gentiles, I did not confer with any human being, ¹⁷nor did I go up to Jerusalem to those who were already apostles before me, but I went away at once into Arabia, and afterwards I returned to Damascus.

¹⁸Then after three years I did go up to Jerusalem to visit Cephas and stayed with him fifteen days; ¹⁹but I did not see any other apostle except James the Lord's brother. ²⁰In what I am writing to you, before God, I do not lie! ²¹Then I went into the regions of Syria and Cilicia, ²²and I was still unknown by sight to the churches of Judea that are in Christ; ²³they only heard it said, "The one who formerly was persecuting us is now proclaiming the faith he once tried to destroy." ²⁴And they glorified God because of me.

Paul writes to the Galatians about his dramatic conversion and his divine call to proclaim the gospel to the Gentiles. Paul wants to make it clear that his experience of Christ and his call to proclaim the gospel were "not of human origin," but were received "through a revelation of Jesus Christ" (verses 11–12). To show that his call and the gospel he preaches do not come from human beings, he describes his experiences to support his contention. Because of the divine origin of the gospel, what seems utterly impossible has taken place: God has accepted the Gentiles into the inheritance of Israel, not on the basis of their obeying the precepts of the Torah, but on the basis of their faith in Jesus Christ. Since this good news, proclaimed by Paul, originated with God, the Galatian Gentiles can resist all efforts from the church in Jerusalem to make them adopt the practices of the Torah.

This "revelation of Jesus Christ," which Paul received, is foundational for his missionary work. It seems that much of this revelation happened to Paul on his Damascus road experience. But it also refers to all that the Spirit revealed to Paul during his early days as a Christian believer, especially the meaning of Christ's death and resurrection and its significance for the Gentiles. God has revealed his Son to Paul, and from this revelation of Jesus Christ, Paul has derived the basic shape of the gospel that he proclaims to the Gentiles. Paul cannot alter it because of its divine origin, and the Galatians cannot swerve from it without violating the divine truth of the gospel.

Paul offers his own biography as evidence of the divine origin of the gospel he preaches. He distinguishes between two diametrically opposed parts of his life. The first is his "earlier life in Judaism," when he was so zealous of his Jewish tradition that he violently persecuted the church and tried to destroy it (verses 13–14). The second is his conversion and call to preach the gospel to the Gentiles (verses 15–17). It is unimaginable, from a human point of view, that one so fervent in his Jewish practices and so zealous in his persecution of the church could then proclaim a gospel that depends on faith in Jesus Christ rather than the practice of the Torah precepts. The wondrous movement from persecutor of the church to preacher of the gospel points to the divine origin of Paul's revelation and commission.

In speaking about his transformation, Paul says that God set him apart before his birth, called him through divine grace, and revealed God's Son to him—all so that Paul would proclaim Jesus Christ among the Gentiles. There was no need for Paul to go to Jerusalem to consult with the other apostles. Instead, Paul went to Arabia for a period of three years. It is possible that Paul immediately began preaching the gospel there, but it seems more probable that Paul spent time there in study, reading again the Torah, prophets, and psalms in light of his experience of the risen Christ. This time of reflection allowed Paul to form the unique way he would proclaim the gospel.

Paul came to realize that the final age had begun in Jesus Christ, and therefore the time has come to incorporate the Gentiles into God's saving plan for all the nations. Only after this time of formation did Paul go to Jerusalem to consult with Peter and James (verses 18–19). There, Paul supplemented his own gospel to the Gentiles, which he had forged through his study of the ancient texts, with the memories of the historical Jesus from his apostles.

Reflection and discussion

- Why does Paul make such a contrast between his earlier life and his new life in Christ?

- Why was a period of study and reflection necessary for Paul before he could proclaim the gospel to the Gentiles?

Prayer

Lord Jesus Christ, you have revealed yourself to me in Scripture and invited me to follow you. Make me aware of your call to me and your commission to make me your missionary disciple. Help me to always be able to speak to others about your life within me and the hope that fills me.

**God chose what is foolish in the world to shame the wise;
God chose what is weak in the world to shame the strong.** 1 COR 1:27

Christ the Power and Wisdom of God

1 CORINTHIANS 1:17–31 ^17^*For Christ did not send me to baptize but to proclaim the gospel, and not with eloquent wisdom, so that the cross of Christ might not be emptied of its power.*

^18^For the message about the cross is foolishness to those who are perishing, but to us who are being saved it is the power of God. ^19^For it is written,

"I will destroy the wisdom of the wise,

and the discernment of the discerning I will thwart."

^20^Where is the one who is wise? Where is the scribe? Where is the debater of this age? Has not God made foolish the wisdom of the world? ^21^For since, in the wisdom of God, the world did not know God through wisdom, God decided, through the foolishness of our proclamation, to save those who believe. ^22^For Jews demand signs and Greeks desire wisdom, ^23^but we proclaim Christ crucified, a stumbling block to Jews and foolishness to Gentiles, ^24^but to those who are the called, both Jews and Greeks, Christ the power of God and the wisdom of God. ^25^For God's foolishness is wiser than human wisdom, and God's weakness is stronger than human strength.

^26^Consider your own call, brothers and sisters: not many of you were wise by human standards, not many were powerful, not many were of noble birth. ^27^But God chose what is foolish in the world to shame the wise; God chose what is weak in the world to shame the strong; ^28^God chose what is low and despised in the world, things that are not, to reduce to nothing things that are, ^29^so that no one might boast

in the presence of God. [30]*He is the source of your life in Christ Jesus, who became for us wisdom from God, and righteousness and sanctification and redemption,* [31]*in order that, as it is written, "Let the one who boasts, boast in the Lord."*

Paul writes to the church in Corinth that his primary ministry is "to proclaim the gospel," which is "the message about the cross" (verses 17–18). He explains that this good news of God's saving work in the cross of Christ is not a message that can be sold through eloquent speech and displays of sophisticated rhetoric. Such captivating eloquence elevates the status of the preacher and thus empties the cross of its own persuasive power. The cross subverts all self-promotion in favor of the self-emptying presented by the cross.

Paul knows that the cross seems foolish in the logic of human wisdom. It represents the ultimate in human weakness, expressing failure and total defeat. In the Roman world, where the cross was seen as the most horrid and barbaric form of punishment imaginable, the gospel about a crucified Savior seemed to be utter madness. To both Jews and Greeks, the cross seems absurd.

Nevertheless, Paul holds the cross at the center of the gospel he proclaims. He trusts the power of the cross to move the audience, rather than the power of his own eloquence. In the crucifixion of his Son, God has surpassed human wisdom and acted powerfully to bring us salvation from sin and death. God has transformed the meaning of the cross. Now it expresses life given for others, hope in the midst of suffering, and victory over the greatest evils.

The Jews believed that if God were to visit this world with salvation, it would be in power (verse 22). They were looking for a Messiah who would perform great works of liberation for them. They insisted upon "signs" to feed their appetite for what is sensational and miraculous. For the Jews, the cross was a "stumbling block" (verse 23). It spoke of weakness, not power; of defeat, not victory; of humiliation, not conquest. For them, it was inconceivable that the Messiah could suffer such a disgraceful and humiliating death.

The Gentile Greeks, on the other hand, sought to know God through reasoned argument. They could not conceive of a man having wisdom yet not having sufficient wit to save himself from so ghastly a death. That God would manifest himself in human flesh and claim to save the world in such a savage way was silliness. They followed those who used silver-tongued speech and persuasive rhetoric, and they found the message of the cross to be utter foolishness.

Yet in the crucified Messiah is found "the power of God and the wisdom of God" (verse 24). In surrendering himself to weakness and folly, God establishes his true wisdom and demonstrates his mighty authority. Christ died for the weak and the foolish. We trust that the cross expresses God's saving work, drawing together both Jews and Greeks who become one in Christ. We trust that the cross reveals that God's so-called foolishness and weakness are wiser and stronger than the so-called human wisdom and power that drives wedges between people (verse 25).

Paul asks his Corinthian readers to examine their own lives and to realize that they are not wise, powerful, or influential (verse 26). God consistently chooses the most unlikely people to show that the success of the church can only be attributed to God. God chooses the foolish, weak, and despised in order to preclude all human boasting. They can boast only in what God has done for them in Christ and not in themselves. This is truth that cannot be argued with reason or imposed with power. Believers establish their identity and security by belonging to Christ and being marked by the sign of the cross.

Reflection and discussion

- What is the difference between the wisdom and power of the world and God's wisdom and power?

- Why does God choose the foolish, weak, and despised to be instruments of God's salvation in the world?

- Paul describes the gospel he proclaims as "the message about the cross." What does this say about Paul's discipleship and the good news he offers?

- What message do I proclaim when I wear a cross around my neck or hang a crucifix in my home?

Prayer

Crucified Savior, who embraced the wood of the cross, help me to hold the sign of the cross at the center of my life. Though it seems foolish and weak in the eyes of the world, I rejoice in your cross as the sign of divine power and wisdom.

**I have become all things to all people,
that I might by all means save some.** 1 COR 9:22

Woe to Me If I Do Not Proclaim the Gospel

1 CORINTHIANS 9:16–27 ¹⁶*If I proclaim the gospel, this gives me no ground for boasting, for an obligation is laid on me, and woe to me if I do not proclaim the gospel!* ¹⁷*For if I do this of my own will, I have a reward; but if not of my own will, I am entrusted with a commission.* ¹⁸*What then is my reward? Just this: that in my proclamation I may make the gospel free of charge, so as not to make full use of my rights in the gospel.*

¹⁹*For though I am free with respect to all, I have made myself a slave to all, so that I might win more of them.* ²⁰*To the Jews I became as a Jew, in order to win Jews. To those under the law I became as one under the law (though I myself am not under the law) so that I might win those under the law.* ²¹*To those outside the law I became as one outside the law (though I am not free from God's law but am under Christ's law) so that I might win those outside the law.* ²²*To the weak I became weak, so that I might win the weak. I have become all things to all people, that I might by all means save some.* ²³*I do it all for the sake of the gospel, so that I may share in its blessings.*

²⁴*Do you not know that in a race the runners all compete, but only one receives the prize? Run in such a way that you may win it.* ²⁵*Athletes exercise self-control in all things; they do it to receive a perishable wreath, but we an imperishable one.* ²⁶*So I do not run aimlessly, nor do I box as though beating the air;* ²⁷*but I punish my body and enslave it, so that after proclaiming to others I myself should not be disqualified.*

P aul offers his readers a look at his own interior motivation for missionary discipleship. He proclaims the gospel not by his own choice, but
because God has sent him forth to do so. On the Damascus road he
was "entrusted with a commission." He is unable to boast in his ministry as
an apostle any more than a slave could boast of his obedience to his master's
commands (verses 16–17).

Paul states that even though he has the right to earn a living through his
preaching, receiving a material award for his ministry, he has chosen to forego
his rights and offer the gospel "free of charge" (verse 18). In this way, his service follows the pattern of the gospel itself. Christ himself became a slave for
all by his sacrificial life and death. Paul's reward, then, is being able to offer his
life to God and to others in the pattern of Christ.

In describing the method of his mission, Paul states that his all-consuming
concern is to "win" as many people as possible for the gospel (verse 19). To
achieve this goal, he adapts his behavior in whatever way is necessary to overcome ethnic and cultural divisions. Paul's desire is to bring all people—Jew
and Gentile, slave and free, woman and man—into the one community of
faith in Christ. To achieve that end, even though he is a free man, he has made
himself "a slave to all."

Paul offers examples of the ways he submits himself to the cultural structures and practices of the people he hopes to reach with the gospel (verses
20–22). When in the company of Jews, he takes on their law-observant patterns of living. Although he knows he is no longer bound by the works of the
Jewish law, he reverts to his law-observant way of living for their sake. When
among the Gentiles, he conforms his life to the Greek ways, clarifying that he
always follows the law of Christ. Likewise, "to the weak," he says, "I became
weak." With those weak in faith or scrupulous in their religious practices, he
makes sure to avoid any scandal, any practice that would make it more difficult to lead them toward an appreciation of Christian freedom. With those
weak in social status, he takes on their lifestyle, becoming a manual laborer
and refusing the patronage of the wealthy.

In summary, Paul states, "I have become all things to all people, that
I might by all means save some" (verse 22). Paul's adaptability appears to
some of his critics as inconsistency or even hypocrisy. However, Paul makes
it clear to his readers that his versatility in ministry aims at a consistent goal:

"I do it all for the sake of the gospel" (verse 23). He does whatever he can to most effectively fulfill his commission as Christ's apostle. The gospel is not relativized to social conditions; rather, Paul himself is relativized in order to preserve the integrity of the gospel he proclaims.

After describing his own motivation for missionary discipleship, Paul concludes with a grand exhortation to his readers, comparing his Christian life to that of runners and boxers (verses 24–27). Paul frequently uses athletic metaphors in his letters, and this one is particularly relevant for his readers because Corinth was the site of the famous Isthmian Games. As runners compete to complete the race and win the prize, Christians should live a disciplined life, focused on the things that ultimately matter. As boxers punish and enslave their own bodies in order to make every punch count, Christians should subject themselves to disciplined self-control and devote themselves to service. If the athletes in the Greek games compete to win a garland of withering leaves, how much more should Christians strive to win an imperishable crown!

Reflection and discussion

- What did Paul mean when he said, "I have become all things to all people" (verse 22)? How could I adapt my lifestyle and patterns of living to help others encounter Christ?

- Paul compared his ministry to running and boxing. What athletic event is most like my own Christian life? What are the comparisons?

Prayer

Lord Jesus, you commissioned Paul to preach the gospel and instilled in him a zeal for your mission. Help me to imitate his passion for the gospel, his dedication to serving others, and his focused attention to the things that matter in life.

**We do not proclaim ourselves;
we proclaim Jesus Christ as Lord and
ourselves as your slaves for Jesus' sake.** 2 COR 4:5

Seeing the
Light of the Gospel

2 CORINTHIANS 4:1–15 ¹*Therefore, since it is by God's mercy that we are engaged in this ministry, we do not lose heart. ²We have renounced the shameful things that one hides; we refuse to practice cunning or to falsify God's word; but by the open statement of the truth we commend ourselves to the conscience of everyone in the sight of God. ³And even if our gospel is veiled, it is veiled to those who are perishing. ⁴In their case the god of this world has blinded the minds of the unbelievers, to keep them from seeing the light of the gospel of the glory of Christ, who is the image of God. ⁵For we do not proclaim ourselves; we proclaim Jesus Christ as Lord and ourselves as your slaves for Jesus' sake. ⁶For it is the God who said, "Let light shine out of darkness," who has shone in our hearts to give the light of the knowledge of the glory of God in the face of Jesus Christ.*

⁷But we have this treasure in clay jars, so that it may be made clear that this extraordinary power belongs to God and does not come from us. ⁸We are afflicted in every way, but not crushed; perplexed, but not driven to despair; ⁹persecuted, but not forsaken; struck down, but not destroyed; ¹⁰always carrying in the body the death of Jesus, so that the life of Jesus may also be made visible in our bodies. ¹¹For while we live, we are always being given up to death for Jesus' sake, so that the life of Jesus may be made visible in our mortal flesh. ¹²So death is at work in us, but life in you. ¹³But just as we have the same spirit of faith that is in accordance

with scripture— "I believed, and so I spoke" —we also believe, and so we speak,
¹⁴because we know that the one who raised the Lord Jesus will raise us also with
Jesus, and will bring us with you into his presence. ¹⁵Yes, everything is for your sake,
so that grace, as it extends to more and more people, may increase thanksgiving,
to the glory of God.

Paul offers his readers a profound and intimate understanding of his own call and his reasons for carrying on in the midst of all the distressing experiences he has to undergo in discharging it. First and foremost, Paul knows that his missionary calling is not something he merited or earned. It originated as a gift of God's mercy (verse 1). Having been called and commissioned by God, he is a confident minister of the gospel. He rejects any cunning or deceptive practices that he considers unworthy of the gospel (verse 2). Rather, he ministers in openness and honesty, refusing to compromise the truth of God's word. Since it was God's action that changed his heart and drew him to be an apostle, he could not be other than faithful to God's mission and ready to carry on without losing heart. As a herald for the gospel, Paul does not draw attention to himself but to its essence—"Jesus Christ as Lord" (verse 5). Since Jesus is Lord of Paul's life and of the church, Paul likens his own work to that of "slaves for Jesus' sake."

It seems that there were those in the community of Corinth who maintained that Paul's message lacked the clarity and eloquence of a true revelation from God. Paul admits that the gospel he preaches appears "veiled" to some, but he asserts that it is hidden only to those who refuse to see the saving truth that God offers (verse 3). These have been blinded by the evil powers of this world, which keep them from "seeing the light of the gospel" (verse 4). The ability to "see" the truth of God's word is always the result of both God's gracious working within us as well as our removal of whatever blinders we have placed in the way.

Paul uses the biblical image of "light" to speak about the glorious gospel of Christ: "the light of the gospel of the glory of Christ, who is the image of God" (verse 4) and "the light of the knowledge of the glory of God in the face of Jesus Christ" (verse 6). Paul is overwhelmed with the wondrous and brilliant revelation to which he is entrusted—hardly a veiled message. On the road to Damascus, that light, the glory of Christ, first shone in his heart. The same God who said at creation, "Let light shine out of darkness," has given to Paul and the whole world the light of the new creation. This creator God has shone his light into the hearts of believers. The gospel is light and brings insight and understanding to those who remove the veil and open their hearts to it.

Everything about Paul's mission demonstrates that he is not the light but that he is a fragile vessel, a "clay jar," that contains "this treasure" (verse 7). Paul's weakness and frailty attest to the fact that the gospel of Christ is empowered by God and not himself. This power within him is demonstrated by four vivid contrasts (verses 8–9). He ought to be crushed, driven to despair, forsaken, and destroyed because of his suffering for the gospel. But Paul's trials attest to his union with Christ, whose suffering and death are being replicated in his own life. He is carrying in his own body "the death of Jesus" (verse 10); he is being "given up to death for Jesus' sake" (verse 11). But Paul's dying with Jesus in frailty and suffering also manifests "the life of Jesus" made visible in his mortal body. He experiences an indestructible power that is not his own, that always bears him up and suffuses his present existence with visible signs of the resurrection for which he waits in hope.

Reflection and discussion

- How does the way Paul received his missionary calling make a difference in how he conducts his ministry?

- "Light" (verse 4) and "treasure" (verse 7) are images of the gospel for Paul. How do these images help me better appreciate my call to be a missionary disciple?

- Why does the gospel Paul preached appear "veiled" to some? Is this why the gospel seems hidden for many today?

- Although there is no escape from dying, if we join our dying with that of Christ, the life of Christ will also be manifest within us. How can I begin to live more consciously with this truth in mind?

Prayer

Faithful God, who called Paul to be a faithful missionary of the gospel, help me to experience the treasure of the gospel in the fragile vessel of my own life. May the light you have given me shine out so that others may see it and live.

I pray that you may have the power to comprehend, with all the saints, what is the breadth and length and height and depth, and to know the love of Christ that surpasses knowledge. EPH 3:18–19

News of the Boundless Riches of Christ

EPHESIANS 3:5–21 *⁵In former generations this mystery was not made known to humankind, as it has now been revealed to his holy apostles and prophets by the Spirit: ⁶that is, the Gentiles have become fellow heirs, members of the same body, and sharers in the promise in Christ Jesus through the gospel.*

⁷Of this gospel I have become a servant according to the gift of God's grace that was given me by the working of his power. ⁸Although I am the very least of all the saints, this grace was given to me to bring to the Gentiles the news of the boundless riches of Christ, ⁹and to make everyone see what is the plan of the mystery hidden for ages in God who created all things; ¹⁰so that through the church the wisdom of God in its rich variety might now be made known to the rulers and authorities in the heavenly places. ¹¹This was in accordance with the eternal purpose that he has carried out in Christ Jesus our Lord, ¹²in whom we have access to God in boldness and confidence through faith in him. ¹³I pray therefore that you may not lose heart over my sufferings for you; they are your glory.

¹⁴For this reason I bow my knees before the Father, ¹⁵from whom every family in heaven and on earth takes its name. ¹⁶I pray that, according to the riches of his glory, he may grant that you may be strengthened in your inner being with power through his Spirit, ¹⁷and that Christ may dwell in your hearts through faith, as you are being rooted and grounded in love. ¹⁸I pray that you may have the power to comprehend, with all the saints, what is the breadth and length and height and depth, ¹⁹*and to know the love of Christ that surpasses knowledge, so that you may be filled with all the fullness of God.*

²⁰*Now to him who by the power at work within us is able to accomplish abundantly far more than all we can ask or imagine,* ²¹*to him be glory in the church and in Christ Jesus to all generations, forever and ever. Amen.*

Paul shows us that what God had promised to Abraham, blessings to all nations, has been accomplished in Christ. This "mystery," the plan of God to bring all into unity, has now been revealed through the Holy Spirit (verse 5). Through the union of Jews and Gentiles, God is forming one new humanity with all the privileges of being God's children. The Gentiles are now co-heirs of God's kingdom, co-members of Christ's body, and co-sharers in God's promises (verse 6).

Paul expresses his amazement and gratitude for the ways God's grace has worked in him (verse 7). Through God's grace he was chosen to bring to all people—Jews and Gentiles alike—news of the "boundless riches of Christ," a treasury that is endless and beyond comprehension (verse 8). This revelation that all people may experience salvation through Christ is "the mystery hidden for ages" (verse 9). This revealed mystery is "the wisdom of God" that is now being made known through the church (verse 10). Through our union with Christ in faith, all barriers have been removed that could prevent us from approaching God boldly and confidently (verse 12).

Paul's wonder at what God has done in revealing Christ's salvation to the world moves him to humbly kneel before the Father of all and pray for the church (verse 14). Drawing upon the vast reservoir of God's riches, Paul prays that God will strengthen the "inner being" of his readers through the power of God's Spirit (verse 16), and that Christ will dwell in their hearts through faith (verse 17). The "heart" and the "inner being" describe the deepest identity of the believer. The abiding presence of Christ in the believer's heart and the power of the Holy Spirit working within are two ways of describing how God works in the believer's life.

When Christ dwells within the human heart, the believer is "rooted and grounded in love" (verse 17). Paul uses both a botanical and an architectural metaphor to describe this life empowered by the Holy Spirit. Love is the rich soil in which the roots of our lives grow; love is the firm foundation on which the structure of our lives is built. Paul prays that his readers will have the ability to comprehend how wide and long and high and deep is "the love of Christ" (verses 18–19). There is no way to describe the magnitude of Christ's love. This love, which suffuses the vastness of creation, is the same love that penetrates the boundless depths of the human heart. No matter how much we are able to understand, all of our efforts fail to comprehend "the love of Christ that surpasses knowledge." The more deeply we penetrate the heart of Christ, the more we discover that vast treasury of love that is beyond comprehension.

Paul's ultimate desire for his readers is that they be "filled with all the fullness of God" (verse 19). The more we are united with the heart of Christ, allowing God's Spirit to work in our deepest center, the more God's divine life fills our own. If we really "know" this divine love in the biblical sense of having direct experience of it, then we cannot but be filled with the fullness of God who is love. This unity of God and humanity is the final result of the work of Christ and the Holy Spirit within us.

Reflection and discussion

- What is the relationship between the mystery of God's plan and our call to missionary discipleship?

- What have I discovered of the "boundless riches of Christ" (verse 8)?

- What can I discern in Paul's prayer about the role of the Father, Son, and Holy Spirit in my discipleship?

- In what ways does Paul's prayer inspire and motivate me for missionary discipleship?

Prayer

Father, I bend my knees before you, praying that Christ may dwell in my heart and that the Holy Spirit may strengthen me. Help me to glimpse the breadth and length, the height and depth of Christ's love. I pray that this love may penetrate my heart and transform my life.

He has rescued us from the power of darkness and transferred us into the kingdom of his beloved Son, in whom we have redemption, the forgiveness of sins. COL 1:13–14

Bearing Fruit and Growing in the Whole World

COLOSSIANS 1:3–14 ³*In our prayers for you we always thank God, the Father of our Lord Jesus Christ, ⁴for we have heard of your faith in Christ Jesus and of the love that you have for all the saints, ⁵because of the hope laid up for you in heaven. You have heard of this hope before in the word of the truth, the gospel ⁶that has come to you. Just as it is bearing fruit and growing in the whole world, so it has been bearing fruit among yourselves from the day you heard it and truly comprehended the grace of God. ⁷This you learned from Epaphras, our beloved fellow servant. He is a faithful minister of Christ on your behalf, ⁸and he has made known to us your love in the Spirit.*

⁹*For this reason, since the day we heard it, we have not ceased praying for you and asking that you may be filled with the knowledge of God's will in all spiritual wisdom and understanding, ¹⁰so that you may lead lives worthy of the Lord, fully pleasing to him, as you bear fruit in every good work and as you grow in the knowledge of God. ¹¹May you be made strong with all the strength that comes from his glorious power, and may you be prepared to endure everything with patience, while joyfully ¹²giving thanks to the Father, who has enabled you to share in the inheritance of the saints in the light. ¹³He has rescued us from the power of darkness and transferred us into the kingdom of his beloved Son, ¹⁴in whom we have redemption, the forgiveness of sins.*

As Paul writes to the church in Colossae, he expresses his deep gratitude for them and commends them for the quality of their lives in the gospel. Through the familiar triad of faith, love, and hope, he tells them the reasons for the confidence he holds in them. They have responded in "faith" to Christ, they have demonstrated their "love" for other believers, and they have rooted their lives in the "hope" given to them by the gospel (verses 4–5).

One of the characteristic features of the gospel Paul preaches is its worldwide appeal. For Paul, this universal, cross-cultural attraction of the gospel is a sign of its genuineness. Another feature of the gospel for Paul is its expansion and productiveness. He believes God's seal of approval on his work is the fruit that it bears. Paul testifies that the gospel is "bearing fruit and growing in the whole world" (verse 6). Likewise, he rejoices that "the word of the truth" that has been brought to this community is "bearing fruit" and producing much good among the members of the church.

Even though Paul had not yet traveled to Colossae and personally met the community, he nevertheless felt a strong bond with them, due to the report that Epaphras, Paul's "beloved fellow servant," has delivered to him (verse 7). As "a faithful minister of Christ," Epaphras had been authorized and sent by Paul to bring the gospel to them. Through the ministry of this colleague of Paul, the saving gospel had been preached and the community had been built up with "love in the Spirit" (verse 8). His enthusiastic account brought reassurance to Paul, for which he now gives thanks to God.

Paul then reveals the content of the prayer he has been offering for the community since he first heard the glowing report of their faithfulness from his representative (verses 9–14). He prays, first, that they "may be filled with the knowledge of God's will in all spiritual wisdom and understanding." These three gifts of the Spirit—knowledge, wisdom, and understanding—offer Christians the ability to discern the best ways to serve Christ in daily living and to respond to the challenges of life within the community. Paul then prays that they "may lead lives worthy of the Lord, fully pleasing to him." The lifestyle of believers should be markedly different than that of others, a visible demonstration of the faith, love, and hope that fills them.

Paul then specifies characteristics of this Christian way of life, specifying what it means to live in a manner worthy of the Lord. First, they will "bear fruit in every good work"—deeds of compassion, justice, kindness, and self-denial (verse 10). These are the fruits that the gospel produces. Second, they will "grow in the knowledge of God." The more believers know God, the more they know what pleases him and the more they desire to please him. Third, they will "be made strong" with God's power, so that they will be able to endure the trials that come (verse 11). And fourth, they will "joyfully give thanks to the Father," for he has rescued them from the dominion of darkness and given them a share in the inheritance of the saints in the kingdom of light (verses 12–13). In all of these ways, Paul trusts that Christians will live in a way that is worthy of their new identity, making their lives living testimonies to Christ.

Reflection and discussion

- Which qualities of this church in Colossae would be most attractive to others and cause them to want to be a part of it?

- Paul was grateful to God that the gospel was "bearing fruit and growing in the whole world." Why is this growth and fruitfulness such an important characteristic of a faithful church?

Prayer

Lord Jesus, enliven my heart with joy and help me to always be grateful for the faith, love, and hope you have given to me. Teach me to live in a way that is pleasing to you and that testifies to the new life I have received from you.

SUGGESTIONS FOR FACILITATORS, GROUP SESSION 6

1. Welcome group members and make any final announcements or requests.

2. You may want to pray this prayer as a group:
   Faithful God, who called Paul to bring the gospel to the ends of the earth, may his example shine in your church to inspire missionary disciples of your Son. Give us the grace to hold close the precious treasure of the gospel, to look to the saving cross, to know the love of Christ, and to embrace his call to serve his church. Fill us with gratitude for the life of your Holy Spirit within us, and give us unwavering hope in the coming of your kingdom where you live and reign forever.

3. Ask one or more of the following questions:
   - How has this study of missionary discipleship deepened your life in Christ?
   - In what way has this study challenged you the most?

4. Discuss lessons 25 through 30. Choose one or more of the questions for reflection and discussion from each lesson to discuss as a group.

5. Ask the group if they would like to study another in the *Threshold Bible Study* series. Discuss the topic and dates, and make a decision among those interested. Ask the group members to suggest people they would like to invite to participate in the next study series.

6. Ask the group to discuss the insights that stand out most from this study over the past six weeks.

7. Conclude by praying aloud the following prayer or another of your own choosing:
   Holy Spirit of the living God, you inspired the writers of the Scriptures and you have guided our study during these weeks. Continue to deepen our love for the word of God in the holy Scriptures, and draw us more deeply into the heart of Jesus. Thank you for your merciful, gracious, steadfast, and faithful love.

Ordering Additional Studies

AVAILABLE TITLES IN THIS SERIES INCLUDE...

Advent Light

Angels of God

Divine Mercy

Eucharist

The Feasts of Judaism

God's Spousal Love

The Holy Spirit and Spiritual Gifts

Jerusalem, the Holy City

Missionary Discipleship

Mysteries of the Rosary

The Names of Jesus

People of the Passion

Pilgrimage in the Footsteps of Jesus

The Resurrection and the Life

The Sacred Heart of Jesus

Stewardship of the Earth

The Tragic and Triumphant Cross

Jesus, the Messianic King
(Part 1): Matthew 1–16

Jesus, the Messianic King
(Part 2): Matthew 17–28

Jesus, the Word Made Flesh
(Part 1): John 1–10

Jesus, the Word Made Flesh
(Part 2): John 11–21

Jesus, the Suffering Servant
(Part 1): Mark 1–8

Jesus, the Suffering Servant
(Part 2): Mark 9–16

Jesus, the Compassionate Savior
(Part 1): Luke 1–11

Jesus, the Compassionate Savior
(Part 2): Luke 12–24

Church of the Holy Spirit (Part 1):
Acts of the Apostles 1–14

Church of the Holy Spirit (Part 2):
Acts of the Apostles 15–28

The Lamb and the Beasts:
The Book of Revelation

TWENTY-THIRD
PUBLICATIONS

TO CHECK AVAILABILITY OR FOR A DESCRIPTION
OF EACH STUDY, VISIT OUR WEBSITE AT
www.ThresholdBibleStudy.com
OR CALL US AT 1-800-321-0411